Three Lives for Mississippi

Books by William Bradford Huie

DOCUMENTARIES
Three Lives for Mississippi
The Hiroshima Plot
The Hero of Iwo Jima and Other Stories
Wolf Whistle and Other Stories
The Crime of Ruby McCollum
The Execution of Private Slovik

NOVELS
The Klansman
Hotel Mamie Stover
The Americanization of Emily
The Revolt of Mamie Stover
Mud on the Stars

MOTION PICTURES
The Americanization of Emily
The Revolt of Mamie Stover
The Outsider (from "The Hero of Iwo Jima")
Wild River (from *Mud on the Stars*)

3

Three Lives
for Mississippi

William Bradford Huie

Introduction by Dr. Martin Luther King, Jr.

University Press of Mississippi / Jackson

www.upress.state.ms.us
Originally published by WWC Books in 1965.
Copyright © 2000 by Martha Hunt Huie

Introduction reprinted by arrangement with The Heirs to the Estate of Martin Luther
King, Jr., c/o Writers House, Inc., as agent for the proprietor.
Introduction copyright © 1968 by Martin Luther King, Jr., copyright renewed 2000 by
The Heirs to the Estate of Martin Luther King, Jr.

08   07   06   05   04   03   02   01   00   4   3   2   1

Library of Congress Cataloging-in-Publication Data
Huie, William Bradford, 1910–1986.
    Three lives for Mississippi / William Bradford Huie ; introduction by
  Martin Luther King, Jr.
      p. cm.
    Originally published: New York : WWC Books, 1965.
    ISBN 1-57806-247-0 (paper : alk. paper)
      1. Goodman, Andrew, 1943–1964. 2. Chaney, James Earl, 1943–1964.   3.
Schwerner, Michael Henry, 1939–1964. 4. Murder—Mississippi— Neshoba
County—History—20th century. 5. Civil rights workers— crimes against—
Mississippi—Neshoba County—History—20th century.   6. Civil rights workers—
Mississippi—Neshoba County—Biography. 7.   Neshoba County (Miss.)—Race rela-
tions. I. Title.
    F347.N4 H8 2000
    976.2'685063'0922—dc21
      [B]
                                                                00-024665
          British Library Cataloging-in-Publication Data available

Author to Reader

This was a difficult book to write and publish, because in its hardcover edition (1965) I attempted to tell the truth about a murder almost three years before the murderers were brought to trial. Moreover I attempted to tell this truth when I doubted that any trial ever would be held and when I believed that if a trial ever were held the murderers would not be convicted. How could they be convicted when one of them was a deputy sheriff and all of them were Ku Klux Klansmen, when their victims were civil rights workers in rural Mississippi, and when all testimony against them would have to be purchased and presented in court as purchased? How could any juror, living under threat of Klan terror, risk voting to punish Klan terrorists?

The legal difficulties in writing and publishing such a book must be apparent even to persons not familiar with laws governing public expression in the United States. How could I identify as a murderer a man who, to this day, has not been accused of murder by the State of Mississippi? To support my allegations, how could I bring into court evidence which the U.S. Department of Justice could not bring into court? Finding the truth and writing it is one thing; being able to publish it is something else. All that is true in the United States is not necessarily publishable.

Despite these difficulties I wrote the book, a team of lawyers rewrote it, after which it was published. As a book it was read by many people; it was also serialized in many newspapers, both in North America and in Europe. As further proof of its difficulties, it attracted libel suits claiming $9,000,000 in damages.

When eighteen men finally were brought to trial, not for murder but for conspiracy, in Federal Court in Meridian, Miss., October 9-20, 1967, the book, as published in April, 1965, was revealed to have been remarkably accurate. Klansmen had been shaken to learn from it that I, as well as the Federal Bureau of Investigation, had informers inside the Klan. More important, the book had contributed to a change in attitude among some white Mississippians toward murder victims. In the book these Mississippians had met the victims and learned that they were not cruel young men; they had never advocated or prac-

5

ticed violence; and they had been murdered only for unpopular belief and activity.

The trial also revealed what mistakes I had made. So here readers can judge me as a reporter. Here is the text as it was first published, and, in italics, I have added testimony from the trial transcript.

The story is not yet ended. Appeals are before courts. Other trials may be held. Other murders may be committed, for revenge and/or to intimidate. So even in this updated edition I am still reporting a continuing story, and at a time when terrorism, both white and black, has become as real a threat to many Americans as white terrorism was to civil rights workers in Mississippi in 1964.

From this edition, arranged as it now is, I hope that readers, particularly college-age readers, can find a clear understanding of this murder. For when historians weigh the sixth decade of the twentieth century in the United States, they will call this murder one of the revealing acts of the decade. It was a planned, deliberate murder to try to prevent racial change; and it was committed by men who called themselves Christians and thought they were doing right.

William Bradford Huie
Hartselle, Alabama
May 6, 1968

Introduction

This is more than a fascinating book; it is an important book. It relates the story of an atrocity committed on our doorstep, challenging our conscience, asking insistently if we know for whom the bell tolls.

It is the passion of three young Americans, Negro and white, Jew and Gentile, Northerner and Southerner, whose dedication to human decency brought them to an early martyr's grave. The rude dam in the lonely Mississippi countryside symbolizes America's sacrifice for freedom along a winding trail that began on the Boston Commons and crossed oceans to Iwo Jima and Normandy.

Three Lives for Mississippi reveals without mitigation the worst in American life with no effort to obscure realities because it speaks from the honest conscience of man. It resurrects from death the meaning of three fine lives. This is a book written to validate the promise of Canon John Donne, "Death, thou shalt die."

It is an important book because its author makes himself a part of the continuing struggle for freedom. William Bradford Huie writes as a reporter but also as an impassioned man. He writes with clinical detail but not with detachment. And above all, he writes of evil in the South as a ninth generation Southerner.

The darkness of the soul of the South will never fully be dissipated until the passion for justice grips the white Southerner. The civil rights movement, unlike many colonial revolutions, does not seek to expel the oppressor: it must attempt to transform him, while it isolates the unregenerate terrorist.

Naked terror alone cannot paralyze a whole people. It is the immunity from punishment terrorists enjoy in the South that endows them with reckless power and afflicts their victims with hopelessness.

Mr. Huie recognizes that the unholy alliance of violence and "Southern justice" indicts not only murderers but the larger society that shelters them. In boldly proclaiming war upon both he joins a yet small but growing force in the white Southern community: those who have decided that social-economic priv-

7

ilege does not compensate for a mutilated conscience and a base betrayal of their democratic heritage.

Nearly two hundred years ago Thomas Jefferson, who knew his young nation had conceived of a new course for mankind, was yet wise enough to face its shortcomings. He wrote, shortly before his death, "This momentous question [slavery] like a firebell in the night awakened me and filled me with terror." His apprehension was then shared by few and the unresolved "momentous question" was destined to torment his country even as it acquired unprecedented strength and power.

Today, finally, all America continually hears the "firebell in the night." The content of the nation's character is being determined in the contemporary tumultuous struggles. They will decide what reality the dreams of the seventeenth century will have in the twentieth century. This book is a part of the arsenal decent Americans can employ to make democracy for all truly a birthright and not a distant dream.

Martin Luther King, Jr.
Atlanta, Georgia
May 6, 1965

ONE

In 1957, when he was eighteen and preparing to enter Cornell University, Michael Henry Schwerner was also preparing to buy a car. At his home in Pelham, New York, he told his mother he had decided on a Volkswagen.

"Mickey," his mother said, "are you sure you want to buy a German-made car? You know about Auschwitz and you know that some of your relatives were murdered there. So soon after Auschwitz are you sure you'll feel comfortable driving a Volkswagen?"

"I know how you feel, Mother," Mickey Schwerner said. "One reason I want to buy it is that it is a very economical and practical car. But, more important, I want to spend my life relieving hate, not preserving it. I see reason to hope that there will never be another Auschwitz." Mickey believed young Germans who said that Germany was changing—that Auschwitz would never happen again. He believed in Man, including Germans. So he wanted to drive a Volkswagen to show his faith in young men and women of all races and religions.

I never met Mickey Schwerner. Had I met him I might have suggested that he limit his belief in Man, that he tether his hopes, and I might have predicted that he'd seek and find danger.

In January 1964 with his wife Rita he drove his second Volkswagen to Mississippi; I first learned of his existence during the evening of June 22, 1964, when Joseph Carter, an editor of the New York *Herald Tribune,* telephoned my home in Alabama.

"Have you heard that three civil rights workers are missing in Mississippi?" he asked.

"No, I haven't," I replied. "I'm working on a novel: I haven't read the papers."

9

"Three young men, two New Yorkers and a Negro from Meridian, were jailed yesterday [Sunday] in a place called Philadelphia. They are said to have been released sometime last night. But they haven't been heard from."

"God rest their souls," I said.

"You think they are dead?"

"Sure. A missing civil rights worker in Mississippi today is a dead civil rights worker." These men disappeared less than forty-eight hours after the Senate passed the Civil Rights Bill. Bull Connor, George Wallace, Ross Barnett, and Paul Johnson had been telling the Ku Klux types that this was Catastrophe . . . Armageddon . . . White Supremacy against Mongrelization . . . the last battle for America against the atheists, Communists, and nigger-lovers. These people had been exhorted to "fight." And how else can they "fight" Earl Warren and Martin Luther King than by assaulting whatever "agitator" they can catch?

"You think the bodies will be found?"

"Not soon," I answered. "Maybe never." It had been ten years since the "Black Monday" school decision. Ten years of terrorist expansion and race murders. It had been nine years since I went to Mississippi and dealt with the murderers of Emmett Till. Many bodies are never found: these people have now had too much experience in body disposal. They have learned from the Mafia and Murder, Incorporated. In their war with the federal government they now plan body disposal along with the murder.

"How about going over there and writing some pieces for us?"

"No," I said. "Send someone else. I'm in enough trouble already." I had written a magazine piece earlier in the year about one of the children in the Birmingham church bombing. Then I went to Wisconsin and made some statements against Wallace while he was running for President. That stirred up the Ku Klux here in my own county; they call Wallace "the great Leader of the White Man's Cause." Now I had to sleep with one eye open and one hand on my automatic shotgun.

We talked on for fifteen minutes. Joe Carter argued that since I had already angered Wallace and his Ku Klux Klan supporters another sin against them would hardly matter. I kept resisting. I was fifty-three, and I had promised my wife and parents I wouldn't "make any more enemies" with race stories. In 1954–55, in the first wave of violence after Black Monday, I wrote the Till story. Then I stopped in Suwannee County, Florida, and got involved in the Ruby McCollum case. I helped save Ruby's life, but at a cost. I was jailed on a technical contempt-of-court charge, and it cost me $22,000 before Governor LeRoy Collins managed a pardon for me.

If you are a writer and live in Alabama or Mississippi, the prudent course is to avoid "race" stories. I live in Alabama; my people have lived here for eight generations; and I intend to continue living here. So for me to go to Mississippi was imprudent.

I told Carter: "The trouble is that after you get to Mississippi you feel frustrated. The politicians scream *nigger* and *agitator* and *invader* and denounce 'outside intervention.' The press sings the same song. The pulpit is no help; it never has been in the South. In 1858 Mississippi preachers defended slavery as divinely ordained, and they still defend slavery's aftermath. Any preacher who does otherwise risks dismissal. So in a case like this, the Ku Klux types murder; many people approve the murder; the rest keep their mouths shut. The whole state considers itself a target embattled against the world and there is no communication, only hate, between the 'outsiders,' including the 'invading press' and the federal agents, and the 'lied-about home folks.' Reason and restraint have no voice."

"That's why you ought to make one more effort," Joe insisted. "You ought to use this case to explain civil rights workers to the white supremacists and the white supremacists to civil rights workers. You are fitted for the job. You understand both groups. So why not try once more? Don't you see any hope at all?"

"Yes, I see hope," I said, "if one can afford to take the long view. There is hope of eventual compromise. Hope, at least, of an end to violent resistance to change."

"Well, here's your chance. If these three are dead, you can show us that they didn't die without hope."

Perhaps this was the argument which caused me to agree to investigate and write this story. Perhaps no argument was needed. In any case, at sunrise next morning, in a white Oldsmobile with Alabama license plates, I was en route to Meridian and Philadelphia, Mississippi.

"What is a white-supremacy terrorist? Make me see him. I can't comprehend a human being who finds satisfaction in dynamiting a home in which children are sleeping, or in burning an empty church, or in whipping a helpless victim, or in shooting to death another man he has never seen before, who has done no physical harm, and who only represents an idea hateful to the Ku Klux type."

I have been asked that question many times, and I pondered it as I drove to Mississippi. I can answer it. I can make you see the Ku Klux type most clearly by describing an atrocity committed in Alabama in 1957—the same year Mickey Schwerner decided he should buy a Volkswagen.

. . .

In the decade following the second world war the national Ku Klux Klan all but died. It took new life from the Supreme Court's Black Monday decision. With no central headquarters but with several regional leaders, chapters began organizing themselves throughout the old cotton South.

In 1957 a chapter of about twenty-five members was organized in the East Lake section of Birmingham. Its most respectable member was its treasurer, Jesse Mabry, forty-five, who for twenty years had been an employee and foreman at Perfection Mattress Company. Mabry owned his home in East Lake. He had never been arrested for any offense. His name first reached the newspapers—and police records—when the Negro singer, the late Nat King Cole, was attacked. Cole was singing at the Birmingham Municipal Auditorium when several Klansmen jumped onto the stage, seized him, and attempted to maul him. Police saved him from serious injury. Mabry, for his part in this assault, paid a fine for disorderly conduct.

Mabry's Klan chapter met each Wednesday evening. Its meeting place or "lair" was a crude, empty, cinderblock building, some twenty-five by thirty feet, located on a lonely dirt road about eight miles from Mabry's home. The building was lighted with kerosene lamps and fitted with blackout curtains. White sheets running on wires formed partitions.

On Labor Day, Monday evening, September 2, 1957, the six officers of the chapter met at Mabry's home. They were Joe Pritchett, Bart Floyd, Grover McCullough, William Miller, John Griffin, and Mabry. A Klan chapter's officers often have titles like the Army: the presiding officer or cyclops is a major; under him are captains and lieutenants, their number depending on the size of the chapter.

The business at Mabry's home was this: the chapter had no "captain of the lair." It had a major, Pritchett, and it had five lieutenants, the others. But it hadn't filled the office of captain, and the officers were holding a special meeting to decide which of the lieutenants deserved to be promoted to captain of the lair. Bart Floyd wanted to be captain. He told the others he thought he could qualify. He said he was ready to prove himself worthy of being captain of the lair.

What did Floyd mean by "proving himself"? He meant he

was willing to "get nigger blood on his hands." He was ready to show his fellow officers that not only could he put on his robe and hood and "scare a nigger," but that he was also capable of "cutting [castrating] a nigger."

It then became the responsibility of the officers to "put Floyd to the test." They got in two cars. In Floyd's car were Floyd, Mabry, and Miller. In Griffin's car were Griffin, Pritchett, and McCullough. They drove off about 8:30 P.M.

Look at those six men. They thought of themselves as "average Americans." They thought they were a little superior because they were Klan officers. They were also members of the "country club Klan"—Citizens Council. All were members of Protestant churches; all said they believed in God. All had grade-school educations and could read and write. Two were high school graduates. Three had served in the Army. The youngest, Miller, was twenty-eight; the oldest, Mabry, was forty-five. Miller and Griffin worked together in a grocery store; the others held comparable jobs. None had ever been charged with a felony. They had no whiskey with them; they were not drunk or even drinking.

The first stop was at a drugstore where Floyd bought a package of razor blades and a bottle of turpentine.

One of them thought of a particular Negro and they drove to his home, but this intended victim was lucky; he wasn't there. They then went to a Negro roadside spot, the Cabin Club. Pritchett and Floyd went in, looked around, but found no likely victim. They drove farther and spotted a Negro couple walking along a country road.

The man was Edward Aaron, thirty-four, a quiet, slender, peaceable citizen, five foot nine, 148 pounds. He had been born in Barbour County, Alabama; during the war he had served honorably with the Army's Quartermaster Corps in England and in the Philippines. He was barely literate. Since the war he had lived with his mother on the outskirts of Birmingham, working as a painter's helper and doing other odd jobs, earning about $600 a year. He had never married—he "couldn't afford to"; he had never been in jail—"never bothered a living soul." He was about the least combative Negro male the Klansmen could have found. His companion was Cora Parker, a respectable woman Aaron and his family had known for eight years.

Floyd said: "We'll grab him and chase her off."

The cars stopped, and before the Negroes could suspect danger the Klansmen leaped on Aaron and threw him into the back of Floyd's car. Aaron said: "Whatya want with me? I ain't done nothin'!" Floyd answered by slugging him with a pistol, then sitting on him while Mabry drove Floyd's car about six miles to the lair.

At the lair the Klansmen unlocked the door and lighted the lamps. Then they brought in "the nigger." None of them knew him or had ever seen him. They didn't ask his name. They addressed him only as *nigger* or *you black sonofabitch*. Not once did they allow him to stand erect. They made him crawl out of the car, then crawl to the entrance of the lair and inside. They made him sit on his knees and watch them put on their robes and hoods. Pritchett, as Cyclops, put on a red hood adorned with gold. The hood looked like a pillow case: it had slits for the eyes but no slits for ears or mouth. Pritchett's robe and the robes and hoods of the others were white.

Aaron, kneeling in the dirt and lamplight, knew he was helpless. He didn't even have a pocket knife. There were no houses nearby: he could scream his head off and no one would hear.

In full regalia Pritchett stood splendidly overlooking the "nigger." "Look up at me, nigger!" Pritchett ordered. Aaron raised his eyes and Pritchett dramatically raised his hood and looked down at Aaron. "Do you know me, nigger?" Pritchett asked.

"Naw, suh," Aaron replied. "I ain't never seen yuh."

Pritchett kicked him hard in the eye.

Pritchett then lowered his hood and said: "Now look around you, nigger! Look careful. You ever seen any of these gentlemen?"

Aaron looked around and said: "Naw, suh." He ducked as he said it, but Pritchett didn't kick him again.

For half an hour the group baited their helpless victim. With curses, kicks, and four-letter filth they "interrogated the nigger." They knew three "hate" names—Earl Warren; Martin Luther King, who a year earlier had led the Montgomery bus boycott; and a local Negro preacher who was then leading an effort to integrate the railroad station. They used these names in the "interrogation."

"Look at me, nigger! You think you're as good as I am! You think any nigger is as good as a white man!"

"Look here, nigger! You ever heard of a nigger-loving Communist named Earl Warren? You ain't? Well, you ought to learn who he is, because he loves yuh!"

"Look at me, nigger! You got any kids? You think nigger kids should go to school with my white kids? You think you got a right to vote? Or eat where I eat? Or use the same toilet I use?"

Pritchett finally halting the baiting with a "judgment." "All right, nigger, look up at me! Here's my judgment. We're gonna take your life or your nuts. You got your choice. It don't make a damn bit o' difference to us. Which will it be?"

Aaron sank farther into the dirt and began to cry. "Neither one," he said.

Pritchett said he'd choose for him. They'd take his nuts. They were gonna use him to send a little message to Earl Warren and Martin Luther King and all other nigger-lovers.

Pritchett turned to Floyd and snapped: "Do your duty!"

Floyd leaped at Aaron and slugged him with the pistol. He didn't knock him unconscious, but he partially dazed him. The others grabbed Aaron, made him pull off his pants and shorts, and spreadeagled him in the dirt. Floyd jumped between his legs and with a razor blade severed the entire scrotum. Pritchett imperiously held forth a paper cup and Floyd dropped the testicles into it. Then Floyd doused his squirming, bleeding victim with the turpentine.

Pritchett passed the cup of "evidence" to each of the lieutenants, and each nodded agreement that Bart Floyd was now worthy to become captain of the lair. One lieutenant proved himself unworthy: Miller sickened and vomited.

They dressed Aaron, tossed him into a car trunk, drove about eight miles and threw him out on the side of a road. As their cars pulled away he crawled into some bushes. When the cars turned around and started back toward him, Aaron thought they were returning to kill him. He crawled farther and dropped into a small creek about three feet deep. The cars stopped. While helping remove Aaron from the trunk, Pritchett had set the cup of evidence on the pavement and driven off without it. Aaron submerged himself in the creek until Pritchett retrieved his cup and the cars drove off again.

Aaron then managed to crawl to the road and stagger to his feet. Several cars passed him, and one of the motorists telephoned police that a "bloody Negro" was staggering along the road. Police arrived and later testified that Aaron looked like he had been "dipped in blood from the belt down." At the Veterans Administration Hospital in Birmingham a surgeon closed the wound and Aaron was given whole blood. For four days his condition remained critical with his temperature reaching 105. He then began to recover, and after three weeks he was able to leave the hospital.

In those pre-Wallace days the people of Alabama were still capable of racial humanity. The press reacted violently against the Klan, particularly after police found the lair with the blood and turpentine in the dirt. Two of the Klansmen,

Miller and Griffin, confessed, became state's witnesses, testified against the other four, and were given suspended sentences. (My account of the atrocity is from their testimony.) Mabry, Floyd, Pritchett, and McCullough were advised to plead guilty and hope for a sentence of no more than ten years. But they insisted on pleading not guilty because, as members of the Klan and the Citizens Council, they did not believe an all-white, all-male jury would convict them.

"You are wrong," they were warned. "Had you accused Aaron of being a troublemaker and shot him dead on the roadside, you'd be freed. But this is different. The law calls what you did mayhem, and the penalty is two to twenty years. You'll get the extreme penalty."

The district attorney of Birmingham is the Circuit Solicitor of Jefferson County. At that time he was a remarkable man named Walter Emmett Perry. Coming from generations of Alabamians, he revered the "Southern way of life," but with one difference: he hated the terrorists. He didn't think inhumanity is part of the Southern way of life, and he believed that a Negro's right to live with dignity is as precious as a white man's.

Mabry, Floyd, Pritchett, and McCullough were tried separately, and the state's case was the same against each of them. After Aaron told his story, the women left the courtroom and Aaron partially undressed and stood before the jury. Miller and Griffin then testified, along with the doctors and the police. None of the defendants denied the atrocity; they only presented "character witnesses," including preachers. Mabry and McCullough claimed limited participation; they said they thought Floyd was only going to "scare the nigger."

A doctor explained that Aaron's castration was a "hideous, traumatic experience in which the psychological damage can be expected to be even more severe than the physical damage." Not only had Aaron been rendered incapable of siring a child, the doctor said, but he had also been robbed of the glandular secretions of the testes which are necessary for general health and he might be expected to withdraw from society and live in a state of embarrassment in which sexual activity would be impossible.

The verdicts were prompt in each case: guilty and twenty years. But for the following eighteen months, during which the verdicts were being appealed, the Klansmen were free on bond, and Klansmen throughout the state, along with more fervent members of the Citizens Councils, boasted the four would never serve time. They were wrong. The Alabama Supreme Court affirmed the verdicts, and by the end of 1959 Mabry, Floyd, Pritchett, and McCullough were in the state prison.

The question then became how long they would stay in prison. Generally, in Alabama, a prisoner must serve one third of his sentence or ten years, whichever is shorter, before he can be considered for parole. Would the Klansmen be favored and paroled *before* they had served one third of their sentences?

In 1960 the State Board of Pardons and Paroles answered this question. The board took notice of the four Klansmen and made a unanimous decision: None of the Klansmen would be considered for parole until he had served a full third of his sentence. This decision was signed by all three members of the board and is part of the board's permanent file.

Thus the anti-Klan, antibrutality citizens of Alabama, led by Emmett Perry, had scored a complete victory. Mabry, Floyd, Pritchett, and McCullough had been convicted and their sentences upheld. Emmett Perry intended to see that they *stayed* in prison.

. . .

In January 1963, however, with Klan support a hate-filled little man named George Wallace became governor of Alabama. The head of the Klans in Alabama and Mississippi, Robert Shelton, boasted that the Klan had supplied Wallace's "margin of victory." It was then assumed throughout Alabama and Mississippi that as soon as Wallace made his first appointment to the parole board, the four Klansmen would be paroled.

Wallace's first appointee to the parole board took office on July 11, 1963. Two weeks later, on July 25, 1963, the board reversed its 1960 position and voted unanimously *not* to require the four Klansmen to serve one third of their sentences before parole.

In October 1963 Mabry was given his first hearing by the parole board. Against his proposed parole only two official voices were raised: those of Perry and Circuit Judge Alta L. King, who had presided at the trials. Perry asked the board members if they were "thoroughly acquainted with the facts of the miserable, inexcusable, planned, deliberate, felonious castration of Edward Aaron?"

"In our judgment," Emmett Perry told the board, "parole for Mabry or any of his companions would be a travesty of justice and a tragedy in law enforcement.

"When we are faced with a wave of brutal dynamitings, when we have not yet identified or convicted the murderers of the four children in church, to favor these Klansmen, to allow them to walk free in Alabama after serving less than a fourth of their sentences: this can only encourage other Klan brutality and make a mockery of justice!"

But the parole board was undeterred. In February 1964 Mabry was free, and the board announced that the other three were being favorably considered for parole.

At this point Mr. Perry called me and asked me to help him "fight the gang determined to free Floyd and Pritchett." He wanted me to find Aaron and publish a story which might help "bring people in the South to their senses about Klan brutality."

I decided to try to help. In the files of the Alabama supreme court I read the transcripts of testimony. Then I set out to find Edward Aaron; and finding him was not easy.

In 1962, as part of an effort at rehabilitation, Aaron moved to a middle-sized Northern city, hoping to escape the stares, the questions, the fate of being an odious or pitiful curiosity. When I found him I was able to persuade him to talk only by promising not to reveal where he is.

In his low, soft voice Aaron refers to the atrocity as "when I was hurt." He speaks of "before I was hurt" and "after I was hurt."

Before he was hurt Aaron was employable only for heavy, unskilled manual labor. His hurt rendered him incapable of such labor. After an hour's work no heavier than pushing a lawnmower, his crotch swells so much he is incapacitated for a week. Doctors have found no relief for this disability. He takes regular injections of a preparation called Delatestryl, a male hormone, and these injections have cost as much as twenty dollars a month. Until 1962 his problem each month was to get enough money to feed himself and pay for his injections.

"In the days after I was hurt," Aaron told me, "while I was still in the VA hospital, I prayed to die. I thought about trying to kill myself. I wondered why them white men didn't show a little mercy and kill me. I kept wondering to myself: 'Why was it me?' I never hurt a soul on earth. I never knew anything about integration. I couldn't find no answer. After I got out of the hospital and the trials begun, I wasn't myself. I got where I couldn't hardly talk, and I'd wake up in my sleep crying and scared, and I'd see them robes standing around me just a-itchin' to cut me. Or sometimes I'd wake up all ashamed, and I'd see myself standing up there in front of all them jurors with my pants down.

"I got where I couldn't look nobody in the face, and when somebody asked me something I couldn't do nothing but mumble. I'd just want to go off in the woods, hoping nobody would see me or speak a word to me. I got where I was afraid even for Coloreds to speak to me, afraid they'd mention something about how I was hurt. And the worst times was when men would walk up to me, Coloreds as well as whites, and make like they was just passing the time o' day, and then they'd sidle around and ask me what they had come to ask: if I could still do a woman some good. I got so I couldn't open my mouth to that question. . . . I just stood there and looked down and I couldn't keep my eyes from watering."

By 1961 Aaron had become a pitiful sight on the streets of Birmingham. Ragged, mumbling, withdrawn, his eyes set back in his head, barely coherent, he was reduced to begging pharmacists to credit him for his medicine and begging doctors to credit him for the injections. Since the VA provides pensions for some veterans with nonservice-incurred disabilities, efforts were made to obtain such a pension for Aaron. These efforts failed twice.

In 1962 Aaron's luck began to change. A good and determined man arrived in Birmingham: the Reverend C. Herbert Oliver. An Alabama-born Negro, Oliver had been educated at Wheaton College in Illinois and further trained for the Presbyterian ministry. He returned to Birmingham and became secretary of an organization known as the Inter-Citizens Committee. His job was to try to reduce police brutality against Negroes. The committee was financed by small grants and was assisted by the Council for Christian Social Action of the United Church of Christ.

For the first time Aaron found an effective friend. Oliver was the man Aaron could telephone when he needed a responsible person to "stand for" his medicine and his other necessities. And with Oliver, Aaron's speech difficulties began to disappear. He quit mumbling. His eyes quit watering and he began to "come out of himself" as he gained confidence.

Oliver tackled the VA once again. What was needed was the assistance of Alabama's powerful congressional delegation, but that proved impractical to obtain.

Oliver then turned North. He wrote to a Presbyterian friend, the Reverend Carlos Fuller, who wrote to then-U.S. Senator Kenneth B. Keating of New York. The result was prompt. On December 10, 1962, the VA began paying Aaron a "nonservice pension" at the monthly rate of $85. This is the VA total-disability pension for a veteran "whose civilian income has averaged no more than $600 a year."

Aaron, with his mother, then moved North, to where his brother and sister already lived. Now he lives alone in a rented room; he has his meals with his mother and sister. He subsists on what President Johnson has called a "poverty level," but except for his years in the Army it is the highest level he has ever known. He has completely recovered his speech, and with me he conversed normally. He was even able to smile several times when we talked about wartime England and the Philippines. He dresses neatly, and he has received a psychological boost from discovering that he has a distinction: children like him. Every child near his home from three to twelve regards him as a friend. So he has become a semi-professional babysitter. He often convoys as many as ten children to the park, and mothers tell him he can discipline their children better than they can.

"I get a big kick out of them kids," he said. "When the weather is nice I spend pretty much of every day in the park, seeing that they don't get hurt. I can't run and play with them, but I can move around fast enough to look after them."

"Are you still bitter about—getting hurt?" I asked.

"Well," he said, "I guess it's something a man can't ever get over. But I don't think about it much lately. A lot o' good luck has come to me. I ain't the same man I was four–five years after I was hurt. I still can't do much work. I can't even walk fast upstairs without having my trouble. But if I'm careful and move easy and don't miss my shots, I get along all right. About the only real trouble I has is, once in a while I wake up in my sleep and I'm real scared. I see them men wanting to hurt me. But it don't happen much lately, and I think I'm pretty lucky. The Lord sent me two friends . . . and a man who's got two friends ain't bad off."

In his wallet Aaron carries two pictures he cut out of newspapers. They are his two friends. One is the Negro man he knows: the Reverend Oliver. The other is a white-haired white man he is never likely to meet: former Senator Keating.

. . .

After I had talked with Edward Aaron I visited the offices of the parole board in Montgomery, Alabama; I talked with the three board members: in a group we talked uninterrupted for three hours. When I asked them about their paroling Mabry and about their considering parole for the others, they told me about Mabry's fine prison record and about how it was their job to try to rehabilitate men and send them back to their families.

"I'm sure Mabry had a fine prison record," I said. "Prior to 1957 he had a fine employment record. He was a peaceful, hard-working citizen. But the idea of any Negro advancement apparently makes him want to hurt somebody. He tried to jump on a peaceful citizen named Nat King Cole. Then he helped castrate a peaceful citizen named Edward Aaron. Have you rehabilitated Mabry to where he can live peacefully with the reality of Negroes attending the University of Alabama? And have you considered how many Ku Klux in Alabama and Mississippi will interpret Mabry's parole as a renewed license for them to hurt somebody?"

I asked them if, before paroling Mabry, they had read the transcript of testimony at his trial. They said they had not. "You can find it about three blocks from here," I said. "I urge you to read it before you release Bart Floyd or Joe Pritchett."

As I prepared to leave I shook hands with them and thanked them for talking with me. One of them said: "I just hate to see you stir all this up. What good can it do? You'll just contribute to ill will and hate."

"Let's hope I can do more than that," I said. "Let's hope I can encourage a few responsible Alabamians to discourage you from releasing Bart Floyd and Joe Pritchett."

I published the Aaron story in a national magazine; when I wrote my first draft of this chapter Floyd and Pritchett were still in the Alabama state prison. But in October 1964 Walter Emmett Perry died; and in a white-supremacy society dedicated to hating Earl Warren and Martin Luther King, his kind is not easily replaced. Bart Floyd was paroled on January 18, 1965, and before George Wallace is replaced as governor of Alabama, I suspect that Pritchett will walk free too and the Klansmen of Alabama and Mississippi will celebrate another victory.

Both Pritchett and McCullough were paroled during 1965. Therefore, once George Wallace became governor, of all the thousands of men and women in Alabama's prisons, the four most favored prisoners became the four Klansmen who performed the ritual castration of Edward Aaron.

• • •

I have told the Aaron story at the outset, in some detail, because this atrocity is a key to understanding the more complex atrocity at Philadelphia, Mississippi.

Do you "see" the psychology of terror at work? In all such atrocities there is a man to preside and a man to wield the club, the faggot, the knife or the gun—like the men who fired .38 slugs into Mickey Schwerner and his two companions.

Do you see the hard-working, law-abiding citizen who gets carried away by his religious hate and race hate and becomes capable of driving the car and helping hold the victim? There were many men of this type present while the conspirators lay in wait for Michael Schwerner, Andrew Goodman, and James Chaney.

Do you see the younger man who, after helping hold the victim, sickens, vomits, and turns state's witness? There were men like this in Mississippi, there always are; and one way or another they can be induced to "break down and talk."

What is more important, note the reaction of the white-supremacy society of Alabama. In 1957, on learning of the Aaron atrocity, the people were capable of profound indignation against the Klan. Grand juries were able to indict; trial juries were able to convict; the state supreme court was able to uphold. As late as 1960, the parole board was able to stand fast. But by 1963, after elevating the Klan's choice to the governorship, the people were incapable of effective protest against the release of Mabry, just as they were incapable of punishing those who murdered four children in a Birmingham church.

The Klansmen are numerous in Alabama and Mississippi. There is no real central leader, though Robert Shelton, of Tuscaloosa, Alabama, who is in contact with the Mississippi Klans, is prominent. An engineering firm doing business with Governor Wallace's highway department found it prudent to retain Shelton as a public relations adviser. Paul Johnson was elected governor of Mississippi with Klan support, and while campaigning he delighted Klansmen by repeating in almost every speech that NAACP—the National Association for the Advancement of Colored People—means Niggers, Apes, Alligators, Coons, and Possums. The Mississippi Klans contributed to Wallace's Presidential campaign in Wisconsin—a joint endeavor by the Klan and the John Birchers.

I don't mean to imply that all Klansmen are capable of atrocities or would condone murder. But the kind of white supremacists who are capable of atrocities are attracted to the Klan—and the "official" Klan cannot escape that fact.

. . .

So as I drove to Mississippi to investigate the disappearance of Michael Schwerner, Andrew Goodman, and James Chaney, I assumed that they had been murdered by terrorists like those who castrated Edward Aaron. I assumed that the murder had been planned and committed by men who believed they were "defying Earl Warren" and acting on behalf of "Christian white men" and the "sovereign state of Mississippi." Had it therefore been a *state* murder? When terrorists murder despite the best efforts of the police and of a society, then only the terrorists may be guilty. But when terrorists murder with the complicity of the police, and when a society supports and cannot condemn them, then the society—or the state itself—may be guilty.

This was Nazi Germany's crime at Auschwitz; I was to discover that it was Mississippi's crime at Philadelphia.

Mickey Schwerner, a young man who wanted to believe that there never could be another Auschwitz, drove his Volkswagen to Mississippi and found another Auschwitz before he reached his twenty-fifth birthday.

TWO

In 1964 the people of Mississippi were about like Americans everywhere, but with one difference. Reformers, many of them from outside the state, were working to improve the opportunities of Negroes in Mississippi—to help them qualify to vote and to obtain better jobs and educations. Here is the difference. Many of the "good people" in Mississippi had decided to allow terrorists to "handle" the problem of these reformers. Medgar Evers had been "handled." Others were to be allowed to "handle" Mickey Schwerner. Moreover, in some of the rural counties, sheriffs had been elected on their claim that they knew how to "keep niggers in their place" and how to handle "invaders." In turn they had promptly chosen as their deputies men with the same ideas.

Many sheriffs and deputies who were not themselves Klansmen or terrorists were entirely capable of agreements whereby the sheriffs and deputies would catch the invaders and turn them over for "measures which would make 'em wish to hell they'd stayed at home and not gone poking their noses into somebody else's business."

This was just about what had happened at Philadelphia. So during the forty-four days in which the three bodies were being sought, Mississippi newspapers asked each day what all the excitement was about. Why were a hundred "foreign" reporters dashing around, libeling the most peaceful, law-abiding state in the Union? Why was an "army" of FBI agents invading the state in violation of states' rights? Why were hundreds of young sailors tramping around in the swamps, killing snakes, scratching chigger bites, when only one of two things could have happened? Either the whole affair was a hoax or the three had been killed. If the three were dead— well, what the hell? *They* were to blame! *They* had asked for it. *They* had come "looking for trouble." If *they* had stayed at home they'd be safe. So what the hell!

For forty-four days Mississippi police, press, and politicians made sardonic jokes, while the preachers denounced the "crucifixion of Mississippi."

Two FBI agents were in a boat, under a blistering sun, dragging a stream for bodies. On the bank in the shade sat three Mississippi "peace officers." They were supposed to be "assisting in the search." One of the peace officers shouted to the sweating FBI men:

"If you want to find that goddam nigger, why don't you just float a relief check out there on top of the water? That black sonofabitch'll reach up and grab it!"

The peace officers laughed. They are a fun-loving bunch.

Here are a few of the jokes the Jackson papers contributed to the search:

The President's strategists are looking around for a 1964 campaign theme song. How about "The High Yellow Rose of Texas"?

Former Governor Ross Barnett speaking in Atlanta: "These traveling agitators have been calling Washington every day, saying they need some Federal marshals to make them feel safe in Mississippi! But I say why be half-safe! Why send a couple of carloads of marshals to look after them when a couple of cases of Mr. Clean would do a lot more good!"

Hitler had his Brown Shirts, Mussolini had his Blackshirts, and LBJ has got his Dirty T-Shirts.

There's a picture for Mississippians to contemplate at their breakfast tables! Old Lyndon dancing in the White House with the Negro wife of an African delegate to the UN!

Bobby Kennedy is setting up a fund to provide detergent for Freedom Houses!

A song by a Methodist minister:

Now the Kennedys they took away our freedom
But they'll never take away our pride,
And I'll always thumb my nose at Little Bobby,
And congratulate the devil when he dies.

Mr. McShane he flew down to Mississippi,
Just as ornery as a Yankee ever grows,
But they made him room with James M. up at Oxford,
So he had to wear a clothespin on his nose.

Lyndon Johnson sold the Southland down the river,
He betrayed his fellow Texans with a smile,

And I'm gonna send him 30 coins of silver.
He reminds me more of Judas all the while.

During the second week of the search I called on the Reverend Clay F. Lee of the First Methodist Church of Philadelphia. I found him in the yard of his big, new red-brick church. He was shepherding scores of excited, happy children onto buses as they departed for summer camps.

"The first fact," he said, "is that I have said very little about this case, and I really know nothing about it. Perhaps it sounds unbelievable, but not one of the eight hundred members of my congregation has mentioned it to me. You see, this is a fine community of about six thousand . . . a really fine community . . . and we have relatively few Negroes. Neshoba County has twenty thousand residents, of whom fifteen thousand are white, and of the nonwhites at least half are Choctaw Indians. The county is relatively free of the bitter anti-Negro feeling of other areas of Mississippi.

"Philadelphia is a fortunate community," the Reverend Mr. Lee continued. "We have three thriving industries along with several sawmills. There are a hundred and twenty-five well-paid federal employees here—with the Indian Agency. During the last fifteen years, while Neshoba County has lost eight thousand population, Philadelphia has had a twelve per cent increase. So of all the places in Mississippi, it seems hard to believe that we have citizens who could commit such a murder."

Lee is in his thirties, and until May 1964 he was minister of evangelism at the big Galloway Memorial Church in Jackson, Mississippi. He is relatively progressive on the race issue. His church contributes to the National Council of Churches, which was one of the supporters of the "invasion" of students from the North into Mississippi.

"I'll have to admit," he said, "that I have insisted on believing that all of this might be a hoax perpetrated to get publicity for the civil rights groups. But yesterday in my sermon I did make an oblique reference to it. I told my congregation that if murder has been committed here, we cannot hold ourselves free of blame."

Mr. Lee was correct on one point: the stories presenting Philadelphia as a dusty, backward, tobacco-spitting crossroads were untrue. Most of the tobacco-spitting is done at the courthouse, in the sheriff's office, and around the jail. By most normal standards Philadelphia is a superior community, with ultramodern schools for both whites and Negroes and with many modern homes for both races. There is little unemployment, and social problems are at a minimum. The major problem is the opposition to any suggestion that a Negro should vote or that a competent Negro secretary should work alongside a competent white secretary. And among all of Neshoba County's twenty thousand human beings, perhaps no more than a hundred are the terrorist type and capable of the planned murder of three unarmed young men whose only "crime" was to make such a suggestion.

"Mr. Lee," I said, "here is an irony which will interest you. I have learned that it was right here, in front of your church, a few feet from where we are sitting, that the three young men were captured. On Sunday, June twenty-first, about four P.M., they stopped their blue Ford station wagon right here. They noticed that they had a puncture and changed a tire. It was here that they were taken into custody by Deputy Sheriff Cecil Price. He called upon State Highway Patrolmen Earl Poe and Harry Wiggs to assist in taking them to the jail. From jail they went to their deaths."

"Is that right?" Lee asked. He shook his head sadly.

I shook my head too. I said: "I suspect that someday I may help make a motion picture based on this atrocity. If I do, I want to come here and use your Methodist Church as the backdrop for the scene in which Mickey Schwerner, Andy Goodman, and James Chaney fall into the hands of Cecil Price."

"If you are right," the Reverend Mr. Lee concluded, "if those young men have been murdered, if they have been brutally slain by citizens of this community who found only their ideas hateful, then we have no right to try to shift all the blame to the Supreme Court or the Communists or Martin Luther King. Murder will mean that we Mississippians must re-examine our hearts and our racial position."

. . .

The First Baptist Church, with a thousand members, is Philadelphia's largest church. Its buildings stand about a block from the modern little jail where the three prisoners waited for darkness to fall and for the terrorists to gather. In fact, as they stood in their cells during the hot, steamy Sunday evening, held incommunicado and waiting to be delivered to the mob, Mickey Schwerner, Andy Goodman, and James Chaney could hear the Baptists singing "Blessed Assurance," "My Faith Looks Up to Thee," and "What a Friend We Have in Jesus."

The pastor is the Reverend Roy Collum, and on the Sunday after the disappearance, in his sermon, he attacked the press and television for what he said was unfair treatment of Philadelphia. He said: "We are being judged guilty in the court of world opinion without being given an opportunity to defend ourselves."

To me Mr. Collum said: "I don't believe the National Council of Churches has sent these young people here on a valid mission. I think the young people have been misled—and that the mission will fail sadly. The young people are being urged to ride white horses and be crusaders, but they will suffer disillusionment and failure."

"Most crusades fail," I said. "Or succeed only partially. I can understand the people of Mississippi feeling resentful at being singled out, made the publicized target for a crusade. But the issue here is murder. It even appears to have been a lynching, accomplished with police complicity. To me police complicity means community complicity."

"Well, of course I don't condone murder," he said, "and it's extremely difficult for me to believe that anyone in this community could do that."

"Are you aware of Ku Klux Klan activities here?" I asked.

"Well, no," he said. "Except that they have thrown handbills in my yard. You know their nonsense; I didn't pay any attention to it."

I left with the impression that Collum was a good man. But like the other good men and women of Philadelphia, he should have paid more attention to those handbills. He should not have allowed his argument with the National Council of Churches to render him incapable of action against the Klan. And if he didn't like the image of Philadelphia before the world—well, he should have taken the trouble to create the image and not allowed the terrorists to create it.

• • •

Around July twentieth I learned that the three had been murdered as the result of a long-breeding conspiracy against Mickey Schwerner. As a worker for the Congress of Racial Equality (CORE), he had been based in Meridian since January nineteenth. He had led a boycott there as a result of which he had been in the jail and in the courts. He had thereby earned the hatred of many, including Klansmen in Lauderdale County (Meridian). The extremist elements—an *ad hoc* group drawn from this well of hatred—reached a decision around May first to "exterminate him at the first favorable opportunity." The other two, Andrew Goodman and James Chaney, had been "exterminated" only because they had been caught with Schwerner. Young Goodman, indeed, as one of the Summer Project workers, had spent only one night in Mississippi before his death.

In the above paragraph note the sort of language I had to use in 1964–65. By July 20, 1964, I knew that the murder had been a project of the White Knights of the Ku Klux Klan, a group based at Laurel, Miss., and headed by Sam Bowers. I also knew that the murder had been done as a joint effort by two klaverns of the White Knights: the klavern in Lauderdale County (Meridian) and the klavern in Neshoba County (Philadelphia). But to satisfy the legalities I could write only that "the elements—an ad hoc group drawn from this well of hatred—reached a decision." At the trial Klansman Delmar Dennis, a Methodist preacher who became an FBI informer, testified that Bowers was pleased with the slaying of Schwerner because "it was the first time the Christians had planned and carried out the execution of a Jew." Dennis also told of being present at a Klan meeting which was presided over by Rev. Edgar Ray Killen and at which Killen said "it would not be necessary for the local groups to approve the plan to kill Schwerner because it had already been approved by the state and was their project."

I therefore wanted to see Mickey Schwerner as clearly as I could see his murderers. I wanted his murderers, as well as the good people of Mississippi, to see him, understand him as a human being. So I worked in Meridian, later traveled to New York, and tried to recreate him.

. . .

It was on the wintry morning of Wednesday, January 15, 1964, that Mickey and Rita Schwerner drove through New York's Holland Tunnel in their blue Volkswagen and headed south. As they drove along the New Jersey Turnpike, a motorist driving alongside might have guessed that they were off to Florida on a low-budget holiday. They were happy and excited. Both were bareheaded: Rita with her brown hair piled high to help her look taller than five feet. Weighing all of ninety-five pounds, she was intense, petite, twenty-two, a graduate of Queens College, thin-faced with alert green eyes. She wore a white sweater, gray skirt, and saddle oxfords, and she sat with her legs doubled under her as she faced Mickey.

Mickey Schwerner could be pegged on sight as today's informal young man who loves to eat and hates to dress. He wore a gray sweat shirt, blue jeans, and black sneakers. A bit short of five nine, his love of food often pushed his weight to 170, at which point he grudgingly dieted back to 160. His thick, sandy hair was parted far over on the right side, then combed with a flourish to the left. His eyes were large and deep blue under dark brows. His lips were relatively thin; his chin could not be called strong; and since he often wore a good-natured, somewhat puckish grin, his friends thought he looked noncombative rather than assertive or aggressive.

In all his twenty-four years, other than in childhood rassles with his older brother, he had never been struck in anger by a human being, nor had he struck anyone.

One of his former teachers told me that when he was nine he looked "mischievous . . . full of life and ideas." In 1962, after a year at Columbia's Graduate School of Social Work, when he successfully applied for a job as a social worker on New York's Lower East Side, his prospective employer thought he looked "intelligent, dedicated, but immature." To make himself look more mature he had grown chin whiskers —the beatnik beard affected by some of his companions. Driving to Mississippi, however, he was beardless. Because he suspected the beard might make him conspicuous and thereby hinder his work, he had shaved it off.

While the Volkswagen hummed along at sixty-five, Mickey set Rita to laughing with his Face of the Month. This was an institution with them. In their more than a year of marriage Mickey each month had introduced a new "face" for their amusement. The faces he tried to make were not ugly faces, but faces in which he attempted to show how W. C. Fields would have looked in various situations. Almost every day for thirty days he'd try to improve on his Face of the Month, after which he'd introduce a new face. To his various Faces of the Month he had given such names as Poker Player with an Ace up Peeking at His Hole Card and Noting that It, too, Is an Ace. . . . Two-Dollar Bettor Watching His Horse Being Nosed Out. . . . Husband on Being Informed that His Mother-in-Law Is Coming To Visit. . . . Unidentified Man at Public Telephone Finding Dime in Coin Return Slot. . . . Y. A. Tittle Watching His Pass Being Intercepted and Run Back for a Touchdown. . . . Casey Stengel Watching Mets Batter Strike out with the Bases Loaded.

His faces, therefore, reflected Mickey's enthusiasms. He thought W. C. Fields was the greatest of all comedians, and he never missed a rerun of a Fields film. He had learned to play poker at Cornell, and he still played once a week in Manhattan with his college chums. He was a fan of the New York Giants, who usually won, and of the New York Mets, who usually lost.

He was born in New York City and when he was eight his

family moved to Pelham, New York—just north of Mount Vernon, where Rita was born. Mount Vernon is just north of the Bronx. Mickey's father was a manufacturer of wigs; his mother, after both her sons went to college, returned to teaching high school biology. Mickey loved animals. In his home while he was growing up there was always a cocker spaniel, and Mickey was the boy in the neighborhood who tended the wounds of all the pets. After graduating from high school in Pelham, he went to Michigan State University. A year later he transferred to Cornell because of Cornell's famous School of Veterinary Medicine. His first decision was to become a vet. But the next year he switched to conservation, and the following year he switched to rural sociology, in which he obtained his degree. So in college he moved from love of animals to love of fields and trees and streams to love of people.

As they prepared for their journey to Mississippi, one of Mickey's and Rita's sorrows was that they had to give away their cocker spaniel named Gandhi. They also had to sublet their apartment on Henry Street in Brooklyn. It was three comfortable rooms in an old, high-ceilinged brownstone; in its spacious kitchen Mickey and Rita had often entertained their young friends with interracial spaghetti suppers amid torrid discussions of the "liberal" politics of 1962–63. But they had sublet this home. They had given away Gandhi, they had taken leave of their families and friends, and Mickey had quit his job as a social worker, all because they wanted to work in the South for a year in the Movement.

In 1964 two endeavors—one foreign, one domestic—beckoned to those young Americans who yearned to help make a better world. The foreign endeavor was the Peace Corps; the domestic endeavor was the Movement. Mickey and Rita had chosen the Movement.

I was told in New York: "They hoped to find fulfillment by helping Negroes improve their places in that portion of our society which still feels compelled to boast of white supremacy."

• • •

The Volkswagen Mickey Schwerner drove to Mississippi was the second he had owned. His faith in Man, including Germans and Ku Klux Klansmen, was even stronger in 1964 than in 1957.

Perhaps he believed so tenaciously in Man because he did not believe in God. He insisted that he was an atheist; that he believed in All Men rather than in One God. His grandparents had been European Jews; but his parents, both born in the United States, had begun moving within Judaism to humanism, and Mickey continued the movement when at thirteen he decided not to observe the *bar mitzvah* ritual. He he was not a Jew, he was only a man. He didn't believe in original sin but in original innocence. Because he held no hope of heaven, he held extravagant hopes for the earth. Because he had no God to love, he loved God's creatures all the more.

At the trial it was this portion of the book which was quoted most often by the twelve lawyers representing the eighteen defendants. Some of the lawyers began the trial by calling Schwerner a Jew, others called him an atheist. Then they started calling him a "Jew-atheist."

Whittaker Chambers wrote: "Man without metaphysics is a monster." Mickey Schwerner didn't agree. Instead he agreed with William Faulkner's Nobel Prize speech: "Man will prevail!"

Mickey was respectful of divergent individual religious beliefs, but he felt that all organized religions, like racism and chauvinism, had contributed to callousness and oppression among men. He seemed inordinately respectful of every human being who disagreed with him, opposed him, or even disliked him. So he was difficult to offend. He considered no man beyond reclamation; he believed that every human being can be reached in time by love.

It is no wonder then that the memorable event of Mickey's college career was his successful fight at Cornell to persuade his fraternity to admit its first Negro member. And after a year at Columbia's Graduate School of Social Work, it is not surprising that he sought employment at one of New York's interracial, nonsectarian settlement houses.

. . .

On Manhattan's Lower East Side there are two bridges, the Brooklyn and Manhattan, which carry subway, car, and foot traffic across the East River between Brooklyn and Manhattan. On the Manhattan side the approaches and abutments of these bridges are about a mile apart, and thirty-six thousand people live there in what is called the Two Bridges Neighborhood. Many people actually live or work under the bridges. The neighborhood includes Chinatown and the Fulton Fish Market, and the people include every race, hue, and mixture that has come to America through the Golden Door or the Golden Gate—or which was brought to America in the holds of the slave ships. Street peddlers hawk hot knishes, potato or kasha; on playgrounds, in the circle of children watching a spinning top, you can see faces that range in color from ebony to olive to almond to ivory. Eddie Cantor came from this neighborhood, as did George Gershwin, Al Smith, and many others. Along with the towers of the great suspension bridges, the Alfred E. Smith Public Housing Project dominates the skyline: many twenty-story, low-cost apartment buildings, with trees and grass and concrete between them.

Occupying space on three lower floors of one of the Al Smith buildings is Hamilton-Madison House; and, from its posters, here is some of what it offers.

> . . . facilities and activities for every age from 3 to 103—clubrooms, game rooms, classrooms, darkroom, shops, gym, auditorium, library and music room.

> The paid professional staff of sixty men and women includes group workers, case workers, and community-organization workers, plus specialists in early-childhood, geriatrics, art education, recreation, music and the dance.

> We open our milk station at 7:30 A.M., our day-care center at eight. We operate programs all day and all evening, and if some of the neighborhood kids get in a jam at midnight, they know they can call on us, and they do.

> [We are proud of] our wonderfully mixed membership, which includes residents of middle-income private projects, a low-income public project, local businessmen, and residents of ordinary old walk-up apartments.

> JACK is still a kid . . . therefore he wants and deserves . . . warmth and security . . . support from adults who believe in him . . . guidance from adults who are trained to help him . . . a place where he "belongs" . . . a place where he is accepted *as he is,* while encouraged to achieve more . . . when you were a kid did you want anything less?

When in the summer of 1962 Mickey Schwerner came to Hamilton-Madison House seeking employment as a group worker with teen-agers, he was interviewed by executive director Geoffrey R. Wiener.

"There was never much doubt that we'd hire him," Wiener recalled. "His commitment was so obvious. But we investigated him thoroughly, as we must do in all such cases. He and his wife had an apartment across the bridge in Brooklyn, on Henry Street. She was still going to Queens College; she didn't get her degree until January 1964. She was also doing some practice teaching. They lived frugally; they seemed to have a good marriage; and neither of them overvalued *things*. His parents in Pelham are comfortable middle-class. His father supports liberal causes. His mother is a warm and intelligent woman. He was quite close to his older brother, Steve, who is teaching and studying for his doctorate in psychology. We found that Mickey had a wide range of interests, including sports and music. He loved life. He was a real doer. He'd drive his Volkswagen all the way to Ithaca, to Cornell, to play on his favorite golf course.

"I had only one reservation about Mickey," Mr. Wiener continued. "I was afraid he might be too permissive. In social work it isn't enough to love people: one must love them effectively and constructively. It's like a parent with a child: you can't afford to love it so much you can't discipline it. A social worker has to say *no* about as often as a good banker. Suppose you are supervising a teen-age dance and a boy comes in drinking. Will you physically throw him out? Will you call the police? Or will you try to ignore him or reason with him? You can't do much reasoning with alcohol. We hired Mickey, of course, but we started him off on younger children rather than the teen-agers he wanted; then we let him work himself up to the teen-agers. He did fine work; we never regretted employing him. His pay was fifty-five hundred dollars a year. With the 'deducts' it amounted to about a hundred eighty dollars every two weeks."

One thing particularly Mickey liked about working at Hamilton-Madison House: his work clothes were sweaters and slacks, sometimes with a sports jacket. His chin whiskers ripened into a goatee, so the kids called him "Mitch" for Mitch Miller, the sing-along man, and all of them liked him.

On a typical day he arrived for work about noon and spent three hours either writing records or making home visits. Sometimes he appeared in court with a boy or girl who was in trouble. At three fifteen the children from six to twelve arrived from school, and he worked with a group of fifteen until 5 P.M. This group discussed problems, studied current events, played games, and did homework. From five to six thirty he dined with other staff members, often at a nearby Chinatown restaurant. Sometimes he'd dine with a case worker and discuss a problem boy or girl in his group of fifteen young adolescents. Many of the Negro adolescents were in trouble because of their home situations. So on five nights a week Mickey didn't reach home until near midnight; since Rita was going to school and teaching, they had few waking hours together except on week ends.

The staff member at Hamilton-Madison House who became Mickey Schwerner's closest friend was a tall Negro social worker named Ed Pitt. He knew the South, where he was born; he was a year older than Mickey. Ed Pitt and his wife became frequent guests at Mickey and Rita's suppers.

"Mickey was the gentlest man I have ever known," Pitt told me. "But he was far from shy. If he differed with you, he never pretended agreement, but he was tolerant of difference. Because he reverenced the individual so highly, he believed that every human being knows what is best for himself, and that the only way to help him is to help him help himself. Mickey insisted that many social workers believe that they know what is best for the people they try to help, and they fail because they try to make people do as the social worker says. I didn't agree with him on this, and we used to have long arguments.

"But what really motivated Mickey," Mr. Pitt continued, "was his desire or need to become more seriously involved. He thought the civil rights movement was the essential domestic conflict of our time, and he wanted to be identified with problem-solving situations. He wasn't satisfied with sporadic activity; he wanted full-time participation. And it wasn't missionary or do-gooder zeal: it was something he needed for himself. He was a young man who had an inner need to be involved with the most serious, hard-core problems."

Every turbulent racial event of 1963 affected Mickey Schwerner. He discussed it, felt it, and became more impatient to try to do more about it. He joined CORE—the Congress of Racial Equality—and in a rotting, rat-ridden loft he helped set up a CORE office in the Two Bridges Neighborhood. He began rising at 6 A.M. so he could work for CORE during the morning hours before he had to report to Hamilton-Madison House.

He had become an avowed pacifist. At eighteen he had been willing to go into the Army if drafted, but he had been deferred, first as a student and later as a husband. Now he declared that if drafted he'd claim exemption as a conscientious objector. At his apartment he and his friends celebrated the signing of the test-ban treaty, which he considered the most hopeful event of 1963.

Twice he was jailed during 1963; once Rita was jailed with him. Mickey celebrated Independence Day by getting himself arrested, in the company of a hundred others, in a demonstration at Gwynn Oaks in Baltimore County, Maryland. Later in July he joined pickets at a Manhattan building project because for years the building trades union had excluded

Negroes. For ten days in July, from 6 to 9 A.M. each day, he and Rita marched in the picket line, until they were arrested and carried off in their most correct nonviolent, civil-disobedient, limp positions. They, along with many others, drew jail sentences, sixty days for Mickey and thirty for Rita, but they were released on appeal and the case was continued indefinitely.

When the Freedom March on Washington was being organized, the directors of Hamilton-Madison House decided they had no authority to spend funds on transportation. So Mickey raised the money to hire two buses for the trip. He said the money came from an "unidentified source," but the source was his parents. In the vast throng which marched to the Lincoln Memorial, Hamilton-Madison House was represented by Mickey Schwerner and ninety young Negroes.

"What caused him to want to go South," Ed Pitt recalled, "was Birmingham. He had been deeply affected by the photographs of Negroes sprawling under the dogs and the fire hoses. The sight of Bull Connor or Governor Wallace on television saddened him. The slaying of Medgar Evers shook him. So when the four little girls were murdered in church, on September 15, 1963, he decided that nothing short of a complete commitment to the Movement would satisfy him. He thought his work at Hamilton-Madison House was too safe and easy. He needed to be where the going was toughest.

"This doesn't mean," Pitt added, "that he thought the white people of Alabama and Mississippi were any more evil than people everywhere. This man was free of hate: he didn't hate any Ku Klux Klansman in Alabama, Mississippi, or anywhere. What he recognized was that the *hardest-core problem* existed in those areas. Only there did white people *boast* of white supremacy and write it on the ballots. Only there were Negroes discouraged from voting, or denied the right. Only there did a governor deny the right of a Negro citizen to attend the state university. Only there did a Negro lack the right even to apply for a job in a state capitol or a city hall. Since Negroes could not participate in public life in Mississippi, Mickey Schwerner was the sort of American who for his own sake needed to be there."

Later, in a conversation in April in Meridian with Richard Woodley, a writer for the *Reporter*, Mickey Schwerner affirmed: "Look at it this way. The people who say it's foolhardy to work in Mississippi are missing the point. They see only the emotionalism in the slogan *Crack Mississippi and You Can Crack the South!* But the point is you can cut years off the fight throughout the South by concentrating on Mississippi and showing how there can be progress even in the toughest state. Of course there is no question about it: the federal government will have to come in sooner or later."

. . .

After they decided to go to Mississippi, Mickey and Rita Schwerner found it none too easy to get there. They were willing to go for *almost* nothing, but since they had no savings they required some minimum support. They learned that one of the new, more militant organizations, SNCC, the Student Non-Violent Coordinating Committee, was selecting a few workers to send into Negro communities in Mississippi. They applied for one of these assignments, were considered carefully, then rejected.

"Yes, I know why they were rejected," Ed Pitt said. "I belong to SNCC, and I recommended them. I knew Mickey could take it. But other SNCC people, at that time, figured Negro workers would be a better bet. A white worker is conspicuous in a Negro community in Mississippi, and a lot of time is lost while the Negroes learn to accept and trust him. Mickey wanted to take his wife with him, and that posed a problem. And neither Mickey nor Rita had ever been in the South. So SNCC chose a Negro couple over them."

Mickey and Rita then applied to CORE. Here is a portion of Rita's letter which accompanied her application.

Since I have become active in CORE here in New York, I have become increasingly aware of the problems which exist in the Southern states. I have a strong desire to contribute in some small way, by the utilization of those skills which I possess, to the redress of the many grievances occurring daily. I wish to become an active participant rather than a passive onlooker. Realizing that Northern newspaper and radio accounts are often distorted . . . , I wish to acquire first hand knowledge of existing conditions in the South.

I have participated in the action projects of Downtown CORE since my affiliation with that group in June. In July I was arrested due to my participation in one such demonstration. I have been an active member of the Fund Raising Committee of the chapter since the committee was formed during the summer to meet our urgent needs for bail bond money.

As a teacher I have been working in South Jamaica, Queens where I not only have had experience in dealing with teenagers, but have become increasingly concerned with the conditions under which these children must live.

While in college, I had some experience doing group work

at a settlement house in the Bronx, where I worked with a group of teenage girls.

As my husband and I are in close agreement as to our philosophy and involvement in the civil rights struggle, I wish to work near him, under the direction of CORE, in whatever capacity I may be most useful. My hope is to someday pass on to the children we may have a world containing more respect for the dignity and worth of all men than that world which was willed to us.

Several letters of recommendation were written to CORE on behalf of Mickey and Rita. Here are some excerpts:

From Mrs. Diane King, Junior-Tween Program Supervisor, Hamilton-Madison House:

> . . . I have been impressed with his sincere and responsible commitment to helping others. This has at times led him to extend himself beyond any formal structure. His views, particularly on civil rights issues, are expressed at times with considerable emotion but with equal regard for his opposition. His personal manner is such that neither his views nor his actions would seem to provoke violence.

From a fellow worker at Downtown CORE:

> Mickey is very calm in his outlook and manner of action. When a decision is necessary, he makes it and carries it out with speed and authority.
>
> . . . He was in command on several occasions when ugly incidents occurred and he handled them with dispatch. On the occasion of his own harassment and eventual arrest, he proved . . . that he is fully in command of himself at all times.

From a professor at Queens College:

> Mrs. Rita Schwerner . . . is a fine young woman, and should make an excellent worker for CORE's Task Force.
>
> She was a student in my class . . . and she and her husband have become friends. She is a lively, intelligent, energetic, dedicated, sensitive, and warm young woman. She was prepared by the Education Department at Queens College to teach, and her success in the program was apparent at every step. . . . In the coming months you will probably get the fruits of all the growing she has done in the past few years.

From a businessman in Westbury, New York:

I have no reservations of any kind in recommending [Rita Schwerner as to] character, commitment, discipline and understanding. I do, however, worry a little about the fact that she weighs only about ninety pounds, and this could be a handicap in some . . . situations. . . . She is in very good health and . . . can match anyone in endurance. But I believe her weight should be considered in [her] assignments. . . .

More power to . . . people like Rita who care enough to give their lives and hearts to this great struggle.

Notification that they had been accepted for CORE's Task Force reached Mickey and Rita on Thanksgiving 1963. They would arrive in Jackson, Mississippi, January 17, 1964, for assignment. They would be given a credit card to use for automobile fuel. Their pay would be $9.80 a week each. In addition they would live as guests in Negro homes, and other Negro families would attempt to feed them.

"I thought Mickey and Rita might have about as much trouble with some of that Mississippi cooking as with water moccasins and Ku Klux," Ed Pitt said. "So I decided I should introduce them to it before they left New York. My wife doesn't know Southern cooking, and my sister has forgotten how. But my mother lives up in Harlem and she hasn't forgotten. So I called her and asked her to prepare a Southern dinner for me and my wife and two guests. Because it turned out to be a school night for her, Rita couldn't go. But Mickey went up there with us, and we sat down to a dinner of grits, red-eye gravy, sowbelly, black-eyed peas, and chitterlings. Mickey ate it like he had been eating it all his life. He could eat anything and like it."

Pitt then warned Mickey that in Mississippi he'd find many of the Negroes apathetic and all of the whites hostile. But neither with the food nor with this warning did he manage to discourage Mickey.

. . .

On the trip to Mississippi Mickey Schwerner didn't stop to sleep. Rita slept beside him, but he drove on through the day and through the night. In the lonely hour just before dawn he stopped for gas at an all-night filling station in rural Alabama. He got out and stretched his legs while a young white man about his own age serviced the Volkswagen.

"I see you are from New York," the attendant said. "You and your wife must be going down around New Orleans on a vacation?"

"We might get down that far," Mickey said.

"It sure is fun down there this time o' year. I just got back from there two weeks ago."

"Did you have fun?"

"Sure did. I was down there for the Sugar Bowl game. The oil company gave me the trip. Alabama and Ole Miss."

"Yes, I saw it on TV," Mickey said. "Good game."

"Sure was. Of course I was pulling for Alabama and we won."

As he stood inside the station, waiting to sign the credit slip, Mickey asked: "Is there any place to eat near here?"

The attendant shook his head. "You won't find a place open for another hour."

Mickey signed the slip, got his copy, and had started out when the young man said: "If you're hungry, I'd be happy to give you something to eat."

Mickey was surprised. "No, no thanks," he said.

"I mean it. There's coffee on the stove, and in my lunch box is a country-cured-ham-and-biscuit sandwich. You're welcome."

Mickey hesitated in the door. Though he had never been in the South, he had heard of Southern hospitality. He wondered how welcome he'd be if he told the friendly young Alabamian just where he was going and why. But the hospitality was genuine: the young man really wanted him to eat his ham and drink his coffee. So out of curiosity as well as hunger, Mickey nodded acceptance.

The two spent ten minutes together, drinking scalding coffee, Mickey eating. The station attendant described further the sights of New Orleans. Then he said:

"I read you're having a lot o' trouble with niggers up there in New York?"

When Mickey delayed a reply, the young man continued:

"That's one trouble we don't have around here. We know how to treat niggers. They stay in their place, and everybody gets along fine."

"Do they vote here?"

"A few of the young ones vote . . . the ones who come back here from the Army. They don't have to pay poll tax. But not many niggers'll ever vote around here."

"What about schools? Haven't they integrated the University of Alabama and a few high schools?"

The young man chuckled. "Don't mean nothing. That's just to get the Federals off our back. Wallace knows how to handle that."

"You're for Wallace?"

"Sure. Everybody is. He don't have no opposition down

here. We're gonna keep things just like they always been. A nigger's a nigger, and he's gonna stay in his place in Alabama. Nobody's gonna change that."

Mickey thanked his host and got back in the Volkswagen. The young man called after him: "Stop and see me on your way back. Tell me what-all you saw."

When Rita waked up, Mickey told her about the conversation.

"I suppose we'll be hearing plenty of that," he said. "That boy is basically good. So why does he need to try to 'keep niggers in their place'?"

A little after dawn Mickey and Rita crossed the Mississippi state line.

MISSISSIPPI

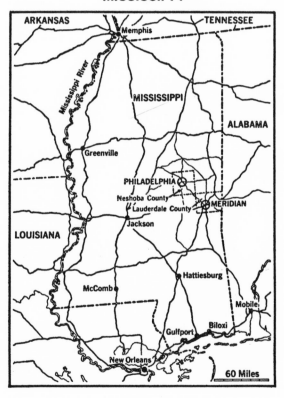

THREE

One afternoon in Meridian a tall Negro youth named Preston Ponder drove my car and showed me the places where Mickey and Rita Schwerner lived during their five months there. We stopped in front of a small, dirty, dilapidated, two-story frame house, once painted gray, at 1308 34th Avenue. It stands next to a modern Negro funeral home. The upstairs contains two rooms, a tiny kitchen, and a bathroom without a tub. Mickey and Rita spent two weeks there preceding Mickey's death. Andy Goodman spent his only night alive in Mississippi there.

Preston Ponder and I were standing on the sidewalk. The house was locked and the upstairs portion appeared to be vacant. Preston was describing the interior to me when an expensive car stopped at the curb and an expensively dressed Negro man, perhaps fifty, jumped out and angrily asked what we were doing.

"I'm looking at this house," I replied. "I'm told that this was the last residence of Michael Schwerner. Is that correct?"

"They were here for a few days," the man snapped. "But nobody lives here now. You better get moving!"

I asked: "Am I trespassing on your property?"

"No, you're on a public sidewalk. But you and your kind have caused enough trouble here. Get moving!"

I started to inform him that I didn't require his advice. But for me to have antagonized him further would have jeopardized not me but Preston Ponder. So I nodded and said: "We'll move on."

As we drove away I saw him jot down my automobile-license number. I'm sure he telephoned the police.

"That's one of our Big Toms," Preston Ponder explained. "He hates us. He barks at us every time he sees us. He hated Mickey."

42

"He's afraid of you," I said. "They've warned him that if he doesn't harass the 'agitators' they'll double his tax assessments as a starter."

The Negro with property in the South has usually been an instrument for maintaining the racial *status quo*. This is not only because Negroes are afflicted with as much human cussedness as whites, but also because the more property a Negro acquires the more vulnerable he becomes to a government he can influence only with bribes. In a white-supremacy society every Negro with property is a hostage.

Until recently most Negro preachers were instruments of oppression. I once knew a powerful mine-owner who fought the United Mine Workers for a lifetime. He "took care" of his Negro preachers, and on Sunday they prayed in church for the Lord to help him and to confound John L. Lewis.

The miracle of the Montgomery bus boycott in 1955 was that Martin Luther King was able to unite the Negro community behind him—and keep it united! The city commissioners had expected to defeat the boycott by encouraging jealousy of the young Reverend King among the older Negro preachers. I was surprised when the commissioners didn't succeed.

Only we, white and Negro, who are cotton's children, understand the effects of centuries of using Negroes against Negroes. The practice goes back to slave days. Contrary to impressions created by Harriet Beecher Stowe and other Abolitionists, on most plantations the slavedriver was not Simon Legree but a superior Negro. He was the first recognized expert in "handling niggers." He used the lash and the salt; he had his own body servants; his "Judas niggers" were his intelligence corps; and he might enjoy almost any Negro woman he wanted . . . even an occasional white woman. Nor did the slavedriver fade away with slavery. Long after Appomattox he continued his lordly reign in the fields and shanties. This is why Negroes, even today, after all the "favors" they have received from "Earl Warren," often distrust one another. They still fear the "Big Tom" and the "Judas nigger."

A "Judas nigger" was partially responsible for the murder of Emmett Till. The storekeeper was in New Orleans when young Till whistled at his wife. When the storekeeper returned, his wife, wanting no trouble, didn't tell him of the incident. But a "Judas nigger" told him—even told him where to find the "Chicago boy." So when I began searching for those who conspired to murder Mickey Schwerner, I searched just as diligently for the "Big Tom" and the "Judas nigger" as I did for the likes of Joe Pritchett and Bart Floyd.

. . .

In January 1964, seven months after the murder of Medgar Evers, most of Mississippi's prosperous Negroes were still apathetic or antagonistic toward the Movement. Only a few of them had joined NAACP. One of these men was Albert Jones, a wealthy, sixty-year-old real estate owner of Meridian. Mr. Jones had gone further: he was encouraging the more militant new organizations, CORE and SNCC; and in Mississippi these two, along with NAACP and Martin Luther King's Southern Christian Leadership Conference, had formed a unified Council of Federated Organizations (COFO).

COFO's state headquarters was in Jackson, at 1017 Lynch Street; COFO was headed by two able young Negro outsiders, Robert Moses and David Dennis. Bob Moses, twenty-eight, from Harlem, with a master's degree in mathematics, was COFO's program director, and it was to him Mickey and Rita Schwerner reported.

How and where were Mickey and Rita to be used? They had several distinctions. They were white, the distinction which had caused them to be rejected earlier by SNCC. They were a husband-and-wife team. Mickey was soundly trained in settlement-house work. Rita was trained to teach young children. So Bob Moses conferred with Matteo Suarez, twenty-five, a Spanish-American Negro from New Orleans, who was COFO's Coordinator for Mississippi's Fourth Congressional District, which includes Meridian and Philadelphia.

Meridian is Mississippi's second largest city; so to the Movement it was second in importance only to Jackson. Suarez, with the aid of Albert Jones, had already done some groundbreaking work in Meridian. He had rented space for an office or a center. This space was five rooms on the second floor of a building at 2505½ Fifth Street, a building owned by a Negro pharmacist, Alvin Fielder, who had also decided to assist the Movement.

After two days of conferences in Jackson, Bob Moses and Dave Dennis decided to give Mickey and Rita Schwerner the most responsible position they had to offer: Meridian, Lauderdale County, and five surrounding counties: Kemper, Neshoba, Newton, Jasper, and Clarke. Moreover, because of their broad training, Mickey and Rita were to open and try to build a Community Center—a sort of Hamilton-Madison House on a shoestring—an activity that might appeal to Negroes of all ages from five on up.

This then must be understood: in the Movement in Mississippi Mickey Schwerner held the highest rank given any white man. His superiors in ascending order were Matt Suarez, Dave Dennis, and Bob Moses—all Negroes. His powerful allies in Meridian were Jones and Fielder, both Negroes. When Mickey and Rita left Jackson for Meridian on Sunday afternoon, January 19, 1964, they carried with them the keys to five empty rooms and a list of young Negroes in the Meridian area who had previously joined NAACP's Youth Council or who had otherwise indicated that they wanted to join the Movement.

On that list was James Chaney.

"We reached Meridian about five P.M. on Sunday," Rita told me. "We parked the Volkswagen on the street and climbed the crumbling stairs. Mickey unlocked the door and we walked through those five cold, empty, dirty, and decaying rooms. But we were both very happy. We didn't notice the cold, the dirt, the decay, or the emptiness. We only saw the rooms as we hoped to make them: colorful, filled with books and the sounds of music and happy people working to become better and more useful citizens of Mississippi and the United States."

One of Rita's tasks was to file a weekly report with CORE's national headquarters in New York. Here is part of her first report, for the week ending January twenty-fifth:

LIBRARY:

Books were picked up early in the week from Tougaloo College, and a small number from Jackson. We have several hundred volumes which have been catalogued and arranged on shelves. . . . We received a large number of children's reading and math texts. . . . All books received have been acknowledged. . . . We have had a small number of teenagers visit the library in the past few days. They seem pleased . . . and we now have about ten books out on loan. . . .

Once we received our budget money . . . we were able to purchase lumber . . . for building shelves. Mickey and several local boys did the carpentry work. I bought inexpensive material and made curtains for the library. A few tables have been donated and we bought some chairs. The library is a going concern, and with the addition of the Greenwood books which we hope to pick up . . . (as soon as we can locate a truck) and the books shipped from N.Y. which we will get as soon as the shipment has been cleared through Jackson, we will have a library to be proud of.

CLASSES:

Classes are a little slow in getting started as we have some fear to overcome in the community and there is a great deal of publicity work to be done. We have contacted the ministers for this purpose and also have placed signs about the community center in stores and restaurants.

There is a voter registration instruction class scheduled for Tues. & Thurs. evenings at 8:30, and a children's story hour which will begin this afternoon at 2. We have contacted teenagers through the NAACP Youth Council, and they have expressed interest in tutoring sessions.

GENERAL COMMUNITY CENTER:

The Youth Council was asked to make decisions about the type of activities they would like. They also have made requests for books . . . and we have . . . decided to use one of the rooms off the library as a quiet reading room and another as a teen room where games can be played, as well as a radio and record player if we can get one. We have set up one of the rooms as the community center office.

I have written numerous letters to sympathetic people in the North and we are starting to get returns. A typewriter is on its way down, as well as typing paper, pens, pencils, etc. donated by a printing supply firm in N.Y. One of our N.Y. contacts has spoken to several book stores who have agreed to ship us cartons of books at their own expense. A remedial reading teacher . . . is compiling material for me. We received a fifty dollar contribution to the center.

HOUSING:

We still have been unsuccessful in finding a house to rent. Mickey and I spent this week living with a family but we were evicted today, with the reason given that they needed the bedroom back. We will have to find a new place to live. Mr. Jones is looking for us, both for temporary shelter and a permanent house.

From first to last, finding housing remained a problem. Five Negro homes housed Mickey and Rita for one or more nights. In none of these homes had a white person ever slept before. In each home, on the second, third, or fifth morning, the same painful scene was played. The Negroes asked them, please, to leave. In no case did a Negro admit he was scared: it's a shameful admission. Each one seemed to plead silently not to be accused of being scared:

"It's just that somebody's coming we didn't figure on."

"We intended to keep you for a spell. But it worked out that we just don't have the extra room for you."

"Things are so uncertain. My husband learned just yester-day evening that he may be cut off at the sawmill any day."

In each case the Negroes had screwed up their courage and admitted the couple to the house. The novelty was a temptation; the defiant act of admission tasted good. But once the outsiders were really in the house, the insistent warnings of the neighbors proved too strong to withstand.

So there were many nights during January and February when Mickey and Rita could find no home willing to receive them. They slept in the Community Center, Mickey on the floor and Rita on a cot. There was no heat, and the tempera-ture sometimes dropped below freezing. Since the doors to the Center could not be locked securely, Mickey depended on his faith in Man for protection. I doubt if any young Ameri-cans in the Peace Corps, even those in the African countries, have lived under more uncomfortable or dangerous condi-tions.

Mickey Schwerner's first recruiting effort, of course, was directed at Meridian's Negro college, the T. J. Harris Senior High School and Junior College. If he was to find workers for his projects, he had to find them among high school and college-age Negroes. Moreover, he had the Jackson experi-ence as a pattern. Tougaloo College just outside Jackson sup-plies many of the native Mississippians in the Movement. Its students help man the COFO office in Jackson.

Schwerner attempted to call on Professor Walter Aaron Reed, principal of the T. J. Harris school. The call was brief. Professor Reed took one look at him, told him to get off the campus and not come back, and slammed a door in his face.

Professor Reed, a Negro, has always urged his students not to join the Movement, not even the NAACP. He once had an NAACP official arrested for trespassing on the campus. When he hears that a student is showing signs of joining the Movement, Professor Reed calls him into his office.

"I know what you're thinking," the Professor says. "You think I'm an Uncle Tom and that I'm telling you what Ross Barnett wants me to tell you so that I can hold my job. But I'm telling you the truth. If you're going to Chicago or Wash-ington, just wait until you get up there and then join the Movement if you want to. But joining down here can't do anything but hurt you and your folks. This is a reality, and realities don't change just because some people think they ought to change. So stay out of the Movement, study hard, and get as much education as you can."

If the student attempts to argue, Professor Reed invariably pulls a letter from a drawer and says:

"All right, so you want to argue. Instead of arguing with me, I'll let you argue with a former student. Here's his letter: I received it last week. This student was here five years ago. He was just as smart as you are. He thought he wanted to join the Movement, and we had this same talk. Now you listen to what he writes me today."

The Professor then reads a letter in which a "former student" thanks him at length for having kept him out of the Movement.

Several of Professor's Reed's former students told me about their having been subjected to "the letter-reading act."

"He never lets you *see* the letter," I was told. "He always insists on reading it to you . . . at great length . . . and his head nods up and down while he reads. All of us who have had the letter read to us suspect that he has been using the same letter for five years."

I visited the Harris school in September. It has modern buildings, a beautiful campus, and is attended by 650 neatly dressed and well-behaved youngsters. Most of them appear serious. There is none of the sloppiness in dress or surliness in manner one sees on campuses in the North and West, or on white campuses in the South. The pigmentation varies from what the students call "coal-scuttle blond" to "pink-toed white." Professor Reed's wife is the librarian, and I chatted with her in the impressive new library. She described the library and the school with pride, and told me of her world travels and of her son at the University of Mexico.

Professor Reed tried to avoid me, but I waited him out and all but compelled him to face me.

"I'm sorry, Professor," I said. "I know you had rather see a water moccasin than me. So I'll state my request, and I won't ask you to say yes or no. A boy named James Chaney attended this school. He's dead now. He was one of your dropouts. Maybe he wasn't smart, but he found purpose in the Movement and some Ku Klux types killed him. I'm trying to understand him. So I'd like to see his records. In particular, I'd like to read whatever judgments his teachers wrote on the records about him."

"Well," the Professor began, "that would take time, a lot of time. Those records are over in the Record Department. . . ."

I chuckled. "Of course they are. But I can wait. And I don't want to know who helped me find them. I want you to be in a position to deny that I ever got them. About a month from now I want to wander around on this campus and by coincidence on some desk I want to happen to come across those records. After I read them, you can have me arrested for trespassing."

As I left the Professor's office, I made a joke. "If I *don't* find those records when I come back here," I said, "then I'm going to tell the Governor that you gave them to me. Just to see how he'll react!"

After Professor Reed had slammed the door in his face, Mickey Schwerner got around the Professor by attending the school's next basketball game. He and Rita cheered the home team and passed out leaflets inviting the students to the COFO Community Center. Of the 650 students at the Harris school, about 50 accepted the invitation, joined the Movement, and became workers. The most valuable recruit was Sue Brown, a pretty and intelligent high school senior. She became Rita Schwerner's assistant in managing the Center; and on Sunday, June twenty-first, when the three disappeared, it was Sue Brown who manned the telephones and never left them for four days and nights.

So from the T. J. Harris Senior High School and Junior College, Mickey Schwerner got his two most loyal recruits: Sue Brown, who was intellectually superior and who stayed at the telephones until hope was lost, and James Chaney, who was a dropout and who died beside him.

. . .

At the end of his first month in Meridian, Mickey Schwerner wrote the national headquarters of CORE. Here is the substance of his memo:

> The Meridian Community Center, of Lauderdale County, Mississippi, *must* succeed. The Negro population has suffered too long with insufficient education, high infant mortality rate, low dietary level and lack of job opportunities. Sure, the task looks hopelessly large, but we must not fail if the South is to take its rightful place in American society. . . .
>
> Launderdale County has 67,119 people, 23,484 of whom are non-white. In Meridian itself, there are 49,374 people, of whom 16,761 are Negro. In the entire city there is not even a "Y." . . .
>
> In low-income areas there are insufficient library facilities for the young, and Negroes are denied access to many of the existing facilities. Recreational and culturally uplifting activities are non-existent in the rural areas. Expenditures for education are far below the nation's average; and money spent for the education of each Negro child is less than half of that spent for the education of each white child. . . .
>
> According to reports of the Mississippi State Board of

Health, a Negro infant is twice as likely to die during its first year of life as is a white infant. . . .

According to the U.S. Bureau of Statistics, in 1960, out of 207,611 housing units in Mississippi, 137,881 did not have toilets, even shared, but had to make use of outhouses. More than 100,000 houses are in a dilapidated state. There is an overwhelming need for housing repair and painting. . . .

In the Center we now have a 10,000-volume library. But we need shelf space. We can't uncrate all the books we have. . . .

With story hours, games and music, we are doing everything possible to attract to the Center children who are five and six years old. These children are Mississippi's best hope. They are the ones who, if assisted, can improve most and contribute most. . . .

We are trying to recruit bright teenage Negro girls and boys to serve as tutors for younger children in reading, arithmetic and history. . . .

We are trying to persuade the local Negro schools to furnish us the name of every student who appears likely to become a dropout. We want to rush remedial help to him. . . .

Each day we canvass door-to-door, seeking Negro adults who are willing to try to register to vote. Twice each week we conduct classes in voter registration. . . .

Pharmaceutical companies are now willing to donate vitamins to us. But we must enlist a doctor and nurse to distribute them. . . .

We must enlist field workers who know carpentry, and who will go house-to-house and instruct residents in means of inexpensive repair. We can provide lumber; and we could organize our high school dropouts into a work corps to lend a hand with repairs. . . .

Above all, we must have job training and *more* job training. Each week now we are trying to persuade employers to hire their first Negroes for other than menial work. The jobs, in time, are coming. We must have trained young Negroes to fill them.

On a typical day in February 1964, Mickey and Rita, if they were sleeping at the Community Center, got up at dawn or shortly after, and went to a nearby Negro hotel which allowed them to bathe. Then they went to Mr. Jones' café and had breakfast on the cuff. They read the local papers along with *The New York Times* and the New York *Post,* which they received by mail. When they returned to the Center the telephone would have begun ringing.

The telephone was a major problem. It was a necessity: for security reasons each outside worker telephoned the

Center frequently, and the Center itself had to be in contact with the Jackson office. Moreover, so that prospective recruits could telephone the Center, the number had to be printed on the leaflets. So the telephone rang almost constantly. Many Ku Klux and their wives knew the number; so more than half of all calls were abusive, threatening, and usually obscene. Most of these calls were made by wives of the Ku Klux for the dual purpose of conveying threats and of tying up the lines so they would be useless to the Movement.

If the lines were tapped—as they were thought to be—this created a remarkable party line, a gushing fountain of obscenity!

I always suspected the Mississippi women knew more bad words than the men, and that party line proved it. Since Rita Schwerner was known to be sleeping in Negro homes, or willing to sleep in them, the Mississippi women were telling her all the various acts she should commit with Negro men. In July, during the search, I sat in the office one evening with an innocent white college maiden from Ohio who was doing her bit for the Movement by taking the telephone calls.

"You must be broadening your education," I remarked.

"Yes," she said. "I'm listening to the voice of the people."

"The voice of the people is the voice of God," I said.

"Then God help God," she said.

I acquired a tape recording of ten minutes of this woman-spoken obscenity. I play it for any of my guests who have trouble understanding how atrocities can happen or why the "good people" of Mississippi can't punish those who perpetrate them.

"Listen to the sweet and charming voice of Southern womanhood," I tell them. "If race hate can do this to a sober woman sitting in her living room, what do you think it can do to a group of hard-handed men on a moonlight night around a corn-whiskey jug?"

Those telephone calls must have had some effect on Rita Schwerner. It is difficult to imagine that a twenty-year-old woman could take such calls for months without becoming somewhat hardened, or frightened, or disturbed. Apparently they didn't disturb Mickey. He dismissed them as the result of religious and race hate.

"You want to kill those people?" he asked. "Do you kill a parrot for repeating words he has been taught? Those people are reacting as they have been taught to react. You change them by changing what they are taught. Love and education are the only way."

By 10 A.M. each day Mickey Schwerner, often with two or

three young Negroes, was out canvassing house-to-house, trying to persuade Negroes of all ages to visit the Community Center and to try to qualify to vote or otherwise support the Movement. If some housewife gave him a sandwich and coffee he didn't stop for lunch. By late afternoon he returned to the Center to report to Jackson, or called on some white employer to try to persuade him to hire a Negro. After a supper at the café, he often went to churches, white or Negro, or tried to call on pastors, white or Negro.

Sometimes he and Rita went to the Negro motion-picture theater. "It was usually a horror film," Rita told me. "We saw *Godzilla* several times." After a day of those telephone calls, *Godzilla* must have seemed friendly.

One night Mickey called on a rabbi, who listened to him patiently, then said:

"I suppose whatever I say will only anger or amuse you. But I'll try. First, let me remind you that seventeen hundred Negroes qualified to vote here in Meridian before you arrived. That isn't many, but it's a start. In some ways Negroes are better off here than in Harlem. Surely you have observed that there is no ghetto here. Negroes live in several areas of this city, and they live next to, or across the street from, whites. Some white schools are surrounded by Negro homes. Even if you don't consider yourself a Jew, you must acknowledge that where there is no ghetto there is hope. Progress is long delayed, but it must come from within, not from without. You mean well, but you are only doing harm. You are young and immature. If you were married perhaps you would understand."

"But I *am* married," Mickey said.

"Then," the rabbi said, "if your wife were with you, I think you might better understand."

"But my wife *is* with me," Mickey said.

The rabbi was startled. "You mean," he said, "that you brought your wife here . . . in this work . . . and that *both* of you have been trying to live with Negro families!"

"That's exactly what I mean."

The rabbi sighed and shook his head. "Incredible. Let me implore you to go back to New York. Go back now—tomorrow—and don't ever return. Go back for your own sake as well as for the sake of the people you think you are helping."

When he left the rabbi, Mickey reflected on what had been said. He was neither angry nor amused. He was only more convinced than ever that Man's hope lies only in man.

"A Ku Klux can abuse me if that's his need," he told Rita. "A rabbi can urge me to go to New York if that is his need.

But my need is to try to help men in Mississippi help themselves. So here we stay."

. . .

After their first month in Meridian, Mickey and Rita enjoyed a "luxury vacation." They did indeed reach New Orleans, not for Mardi Gras, but a week later.

"It was wonderful," Rita recalled. "Like a dream now. A meeting of the Southern CORE staff. Mickey and I drove to Jackson; from there three carloads of us drove to New Orleans to join about fifty other CORE workers. We were all so excited, and we had so much to talk about. And what luxury! CORE had rented a new, very modern, Negro motel, with beautiful rooms, TV, and private baths. We spent four glorious nights there, talking and planning day and night, and stretching out on those soft mattresses and relaxing in those bathtubs. On Saturday night some of us went out on the town for fun . . . to the French Quarter. There were about eight or ten of us, half white and half Negro, and all we wanted was to splurge on a luxury meal in one of the fine restaurants. Then we wanted to hear some real New Orleans jazz. The last thing we wanted was to get arrested or cause any trouble.

"Well, we walked through the French Quarter, but every restaurant and night club turned us away. We were disappointed, but we didn't try to stage any demonstrations. We just came back to the motel, with sandwiches and coffee, and talked most of the night. Next day we drove back to Jackson and Meridian determined to work twice as hard."

FOUR

By March 1, 1964, Mickey and Rita Schwerner felt that they had their feet on the ground in Meridian. They thought they were getting somewhere. Here is an excerpt from their reports:

> . . . we have rented a house at a cost of $9 a week. It has four large, clean rooms and will house a considerable number of people. We bought second hand beds and mattresses, and other essentials and I have made curtains for the windows. The address is 306 44th Avenue. We do not yet have a phone as the telephone company has been giving us opposition. Matt Suarez and Mickey spoke to the manager yesterday, and we are hopeful of getting a phone installed shortly.

I visited this house. It is painted yellow, is kept in good repair, and has a complete bathroom. It is in an all-Negro neighborhood, but the owner is white. It became a Freedom House for three months by a ruse. Albert Jones rented it himself from the white owner, then sublet it to Mickey and Rita. Almost immediately thereafter the white owner began to feel pressure, but Mickey and Rita were not forced out until the last week in May when water, gas, and electricity were cut off.

> The children's story hour is growing in size and popularity. Today we have about fifteen youngsters here for the afternoon. I read to them, we selected books which we read together, we sang several songs (freedom songs were in demand) and they all left clutching books. . . .
> Our system of loaning books for periods of two weeks is working well. Even our littlest visitors have returned their books on time and taken out new ones. . . .
> Yesterday the priest of the Negro parish in Meridian paid

54

us a visit. I had attended services at his church two Sundays ago. He was interested in the center and said he would urge his parishioners to make use of it. We discussed the problem of integrating the Catholic churches in this city. He is very soft spoken and probably will not be a crusader, yet he believes we are morally correct and may quietly support us. . . .

Our relations with local Negroes who have influence remain uncertain. A few of them are helpful. Others are hypocritical. They pretend to be friendly, but they really don't want us here. Still others remain openly hostile. . . .

The white community remains quietly hostile. The hostility has not taken the form of arrests or even our being picked up. There are just a lot of small inconveniences like long delays in getting telephones.

Fear is holding the entire city back.

The reason Mickey and Rita had not been arrested, or physically abused, is significant. The power structure in Meridian controls the police. The police are *told,* and they do as they are told, or they get fired and have trouble getting other jobs. Moreover, they have trouble renting houses or getting their own water and electricity turned on.

The men with the power in Mississippi's major cities—Jackson, Meridian, and Biloxi—are not Ku Klux or terrorists. They are as contemptuous of Ku Klux as they are of Mickey Schwerner and Martin Luther King and the average cop. They expect to survive them all.

The power structure in Jackson loathed Byron de la Beckwith. They wanted him in the gas chamber and nearly succeeded. In due course they'll drive him out of Mississippi, just as in due course they drove out the murderers of Emmett Till, and just as in due course they'll drive out the murderers of Mickey Schwerner.

So Mickey and Rita could sleep safely in Meridian, or walk or drive down streets safely, for one specific reason; the police had been *ordered* not to harm them, and the police had been *ordered* to see that no Ku Klux harmed them.

The smart way to resist "agitators" in Mississippi is not to break their heads but to protect them and let time and circumstance break their hearts. The men with the power in Mississippi know this. Only the peckerwood politicians and the jerks in the backwoods don't know it. This is why the prosperous, growing cities of Jackson, Meridian, and Biloxi are relatively safe for "agitators"—and why most of the violence occurs in places like Philadelphia and McComb. Violence is bad business.

Mickey Schwerner lived five months in Meridian without a hand being raised against him. He walked and rode down dark streets unmolested. Had he remained in Lauderdale County and not ventured into the rural counties, he'd be alive today.

Rita Schwerner reports:

. . . We integrated our first white church last Sunday. The white minister had invited us, and Mickey and I went with two Negro girls. We were seated without incident, and all we had to endure was some blank and hostile stares. But now the reaction has set in. Members of the congregation have threatened to leave the church, and an effort is under way to oust the minister. A vindictive editorial appeared in the Meridian paper. The gist of the editorial is that outsiders alone are not to blame for integration, but that local people are to blame if they fail to take a stand when members of "another race" invade their church. The paper has urged members of the church to oust the minister and any members who are responsible. After the editorial appeared, Mickey telephoned the minister to express our concern for him, but also to make clear that we believe in the moral rightness of our action. The minister appeared to appreciate the call and said that he, too, believed that the action had been correct, and that the congregation would have to learn to accept integration. . . .

Yesterday [March 13th] the police picked up Mickey. This is the first time since we have been in Meridian that the police have bothered us. He was at the book counter of one of the chain stores when a plain clothes detective approached him and asked him to come to the police station. Mickey asked what he was charged with and the answer was: "Nothing now but I will charge you." At the station Mickey was questioned for a few minutes, asked to show his identification, and was released without being charged. We believe that this harassment is due to nervousness built up in town because of our church visit. We expect more similar treatment in the near future.

The Schwerners were constantly looking for new ways to build up the Center and work with the Negro community. Money, as always, remained a problem:

. . . We have at last managed to get a sewing machine, and we promptly distributed a leaflet announcing it. This has attracted a number of women to the Center whom we could not otherwise appeal to. Some of these women have come up to sew, and others are selecting material and buying patterns to begin sewing. . . .

We have received a list of films which can be ordered at a small fee through the Anti-Defamation League. We are going through the list to see if we can find appropriate ones for showing here.

We are extremely short of money and have had to postpone action on some phases of operation due to budget limitations. Since we have not been reimbursed for any food, we have been forced to pay some of these bills both from our $10 weekly and from money we had allotted for budget. When people passing through Meridian stop at Freedom House, our food money is even further strained.

When spring came to Meridian, Mickey and Rita were sharing the yellow Freedom House with two young Negroes, Preston Ponder and Lenora Thurmond. Preston was nineteen and a graduate of Rowan High School of Hattiesburg. His father is the Reverend L. P. Ponder, a Methodist minister in Hattiesburg, himself active in the Movement. Lenora was twenty-one, pretty and honey-colored, from Lexington, Mississippi. Preston worked with Mickey in canvassing, while Lenora worked with Rita and Sue Brown at the Center.

"We were extremely careful about the conduct of all the workers who stayed at Freedom House," Rita told me. "No drinking of any sort was tolerated, nor was sexual indiscretion. We were under constant attack for alleged sexual looseness: you could pick up the telephone at the Center at any hour and listen to descriptions of imaginary orgies at Freedom Houses. We had strict rules governing personal conduct. We constantly emphasized to the workers what they knew already: that we could not afford to hurt the Movement with personal misconduct."

Preston Ponder gave me his recollections of Mickey.

"He was a very relaxed man to work with. He was always bareheaded, and he wore his sweat shirt, blue jeans, and black sneakers. He had no concern for personal appearance. He let two young Negroes who were studying to be barbers cut his hair. He let his beard grow out again. He said that he had decided that all the people who hated him were going to hate him anyway, beard or not, so he might as well wear it. Sometimes we'd buy food and take it to the Freedom House for Rita and Lenora to cook. We'd have to be careful where we shopped because the supermarkets would run the prices up on us. I once picked up a jar of peanut butter that was marked thirty-nine cents. When I got to the checkout man, he said the price had gone up to a dollar twenty-five. I put it back and walked out. Mickey liked for Rita to fry pancakes for him to eat with plenty of syrup. But usually we just had soda pop and bread to eat at night with maybe a little cheese."

Insults shouted at him never bothered Mickey. On his way to the Center he often encountered people who called him names and baited him with a variety of epithets. One morning the dialogue went like this:

"Hi, Jew-boy."

"Hi, Doe."

"How's the nigger-loving going, Jew-boy?"

"How're things with you, Doe?"

"You're not supposed to call me Doe, Jew-boy. You're supposed to call me *Mister* Doe."

"Okay, I'll call you Mister Doe."

"You will?"

"Sure. I'll call you Mister Doe. If you'll call me Mister Jew-boy."

On the Sunday when the murderers gathered in the moonlight, waiting for Mickey and his companions to be delivered to them, Does were there. They still wanted the "Jew-boy" to call them Mister.

. . .

On April 23, 1964, this letter was addressed to the national office of CORE:

We're writing to . . . ask a favor. We know that CORE is short of funds, and therefore we debated a long time before bringing up this subject . . . but we feel that it is important. We would like to . . . implore the National Office to place a young man on field staff.

James Chaney is 21 and a native of Meridian. Since the office was established here, long before any of the three of us arrived in town, he has been working full time, doing whatever work was necessary. When he started to get the community center in order, James worked with Mick building shelves, loading books, painting. He has canvassed, set up meetings, gone out into some of the rough rural counties to make contacts for us. Tonite he is running a mass meeting here in Meridian. In short, there is no distinction in our minds or his as to the amount of work he should do as a volunteer, and we as paid staff. We consider James part of the Meridian staff, and he is in on all major decisions which are made here.

In February, when there was so much work to be done in Canton, Matt Suarez asked for help and James went. He worked in Canton for almost a month, helping to organize for Freedom Day. He spent about a week in Greenwood, prior to the Freedom Day there. He was sent into Carthage, and would have continued to do voter registration work there, though only a volunteer, had it not been decided to temporarily abandon that spot.

James has never so much as asked us to buy him a cup of coffee, though he has no means of support. We believe that since he long ago accepted the responsibilities of a CORE staff person, he should be given now the rights and privileges which go along with the job.

Thank you for listening to our request. . . .

For freedom,
(signed) *Rita and Mike Schwerner*
Lenora Thurmond

Sue Brown gave me these further comments on James Chaney:

"I remember seeing him in high school before he dropped out. He was the typical young Mississippi Negro, from a broken home, who becomes a dropout. His father was gone; his mother had five children; and they all tried to do what they could to keep bread on the table. He didn't have much to say, and he always walked with his head down. He did odd jobs, like a painter's helper or a carpenter's helper. He knew he wasn't going anywhere. His speech was crude: he used words like *ain't*. So he was the kind the Movement means everything to. He got so he could get up before a small crowd and urge them to join the Movement. He'd go hungry and do all the dirty work, just for the chance to stay around the Center where he felt like something was going on. I guess with the Movement he found his first sense of participation. Mickey knew how to put him at his ease, so Mickey could count on Jim Chaney to walk through hell with him."

Jim Chaney typifies those Southern Negroes who found in the Movement a chance to make their lives count. Outside the Movement he was Nobody facing a lifetime of being a "boy" helper to a white carpenter or painter or plumber. Inside the Movement he was Somebody; people would listen to him and he had something to contribute. The white-supremacy terrorists might scare Jim Chaney. But the only way they could stop his "agitatin'" was to pump three .38 slugs into him.

The coming of spring put Mickey Schwerner on a spot. The time had come for him to produce. And by producing I mean he had to place at least one Negro in a better and *visible* job. To Southern Negroes this is the decisive proof of the Movement. A Negro's qualifying to vote in Mississippi is important psychologically and as one of several means to an

end. But it doesn't put more meat on his table. At least not
now . . . and *now* is a Movement promise.

A Negro child's entering a previously all-white school is
important psychologically and as another means to the end. It
shows the whites that the sky doesn't fall when it happens;
and it shows the Negroes that it can be done. But in fact it
often leads to nothing more than disillusionment. The
Negroes, naturally, have come to believe that school integration will bring miraculous change. Hopes span too high. The
morning after integration brings the realization that for
whites as well as for Negroes life is tough and tragic, and a
Negro child's entering a white school only means he will have
to work harder.

So the best proof of a better day is a better job for one
Negro—then two, then three. A Negro being allowed to eat
at a Woolworth's lunch counter is important, but far less important than a Negro girl standing behind a Woolworth counter doing the same work for the same wages as white girls. A
neatly dressed, efficient Negro man or woman standing in a
bank cage in Mississippi, counting out money, can be worth
more than ten thousand new Negro voters. The day such a
bank teller becomes visible will be the day a white-supremacy
society really begins to change.

What is needed is the *visible* Negro employee in businesses
not limited to Negro customers. Stores and banks in Mississippi have always employed Negroes, but they have kept the
Negroes invisible. Negroes have worked in the back rooms;
they have come up front to sweep and mop after the doors
have been closed. The Movement, in effect, aims at visibility.

"Of course we understood this," Rita Schwerner explained.
"We had been telling the Negroes that they could influence
their own destiny, and the time had come for us to try to
prove it. The principal cause of Negro apathy is that Negroes
don't really believe they can change things. We had been telling the Meridian Negroes that they could effect change, that
we could help them to help themselves, that if only they
would work and take the risks, they *could* assure better job
opportunities for their children."

The initial objective was simple: to place one Negro behind one counter in one variety store in Meridian.

To achieve such an objective you first must have the one
Negro who can and will fill the job if you can get it for her.
So for weeks Mickey and Rita had been working with a
young Negro woman, preparing her to become a clerk in a
variety store. In addition to preparing her to do the work,
they also had to prepare her to assume the risks and accept

the insults. Then they picked the store: a variety store about
a block from the Community Center. Most of its sales were
to Negroes, yet it had no visible Negro employee. It was
therefore a limited objective, but a very important one, and
one that they believed could be attained.

"Both Mickey and I called on the manager," Rita said.
"We wanted to persuade him to break the ice and hire our
candidate for his first Negro clerk. But he was a young man
who figured that if he did nothing his troubles would go
away. He made the usual excuses. He thought he couldn't
afford to put a Negro behind a counter . . . that if he did
he'd have trouble with his white employees, he'd be boycotted
by his white customers, and probably burned out or dynamited. He thought we were trying to ruin his business and
that we ought to pick on somebody bigger than he was."

I later called on this store manager. "I'm sorry they killed
the Jew-boy with the beard," he said. "He wasn't a bad guy.
But him and his little wife just didn't understand. Hell, I like
niggers. I know how to work 'em; I do business with 'em. I
think too much of a good nigger to want to put a nice nigger
gal in here behind a counter where all she'd hear all day long
is a stream of filth. You know what these white women
would walk up to her and say under their breath. And you
know how easy it is to break one of those big plate-glass windows. Two young punks can drive by in a pickup at midnight
and flip a steel ball through a window with a flipper. No risk
at all. Except it costs me a lot of money. Hell, it's just common sense not to put niggers behind counters until everybody
else does."

"I can answer one question for you," I said. "You once
asked him why he didn't first pick on Woolworth's and Kress'
instead of you. The answer is that he was a small operator,
too. He wasn't yet big enough to take on the big ones. He
had to start with somebody nearer his size."

To fight his first battle Mickey had about fifty troops. He
called them "the kids." They were young Negroes from four-
teen to twenty-one and, like a football coach building team
spirit, he dressed them out in new T-shirts with FREEDOM
NOW across their chests. He planned to use them to picket the
store as well as to distribute leaflets in which he urged all the
Negroes in Lauderdale County to join a boycott until the
store agreed to hire its first visible Negro.

The battle was to begin on a Saturday, the traditional big-
business day in the South, when the country folks come to
town to trade. For two weeks preceding D-Day, April 25,
there was a mass meeting every night, either at the Center or

at some Negro church. The speakers were Mickey and Lenora Thurmond and Preston Ponder and Jim Chaney, and
they all emphasized discipline, good conduct, and nonviolence. The troops were instructed in how not to lose their
heads when cursed and taunted, how not to fight back if
struck. They played a game called Redneck-and-Nigger. They
would choose up and one group would be Rednecks, the others would be Niggers. Then the Niggers would try to see how
long they could remain "good-natured and smiling" while the
Rednecks jostled them and called them "black-assed coons."

The first day of the battle was noisy and successful. Traffic
jammed the street as drivers slowed to watch the excitement.
The police whistled and waved them on. Groups of white
youths jostled the pickets and taunted them.

"You know what the Governor said about'cha, don'tcha?
NAACP—Niggers, Apes, Alligators, Coons, and Possums!
NAACP! Niggers, Apes, Alligators, Coons, and Possums!"

The police did nothing but keep order. Not one of them
even spoke to Mickey Schwerner. They chewed their tobacco
and moved in only when a blow appeared imminent. Not one
Negro entered the store which obviously was doing less than
half a normal Saturday's business. Mickey and "the kids"
were elated at the week-end mass meetings.

But Monday was a different story. Few people were in
town when the police quietly arrested Mickey and Lenora
Thurmond. The charge against Mickey: blocking a crosswalk.

At the jail Mickey requested that he be placed in the
"tank" with Negro males instead of with whites. The jailer
replied: "You're in our house now, boy. We'll decide where
to put you. You'll go in with the whites."

Mickey assumed that this meant he would be beaten up in
jail. He had heard stories of how cops invite white prisoners
to "handle" nigger-lovers and "work them over." So when he
was locked in with a dozen white men, he expected only epithets and blows. But no blows fell. The toughest-looking
white man said to him quietly: "Keep your mouth shut, boy.
I know who you are and what you been doing. But the others
don't know much. So keep your mouth shut and I'll see you
don't get hurt. I don't think you're a sonofabitch. I just think
you're a goddam fool. Lot of fools in the world."

On Monday night, while Mickey and the others were in
jail, there was another mass meeting at which Rita and those
who had not been arrested tried to use the excitement to persuade more Negroes to support the Movement. An NAACP
lawyer from Atlanta was present, seeking a "constitutional

issue" in the case to contest. But "blocking a crosswalk" is a charge difficult to take to the Supreme Court. Only Lenora Thurmond had been charged with an offense which might be challengeable. For some reason the police had charged her alone with "interfering with a man's business."

On Tuesday Mickey and Lenora were still in jail, and the lawyer wanted Lenora to stay in jail so he could make an issue of her case. But Rita Schwerner, on a visit to the jail, decided that Lenora should not stay. A pretty, honey-colored Negro girl runs even more risks in a Mississippi jail than a "nigger-loving Jew-boy."

I make no charges against the jailers in Meridian or Lauderdale County. I think their jails are safely and fairly operated. But, in truth, I once knew a sheriff who staged regular "entertainments" in his jail. After inviting several friends to the show, he would lock a Negro girl prisoner in a cell with a particularly aggressive Negro male who "hadn't been on a woman for a week or more." With the bully-boy types the resulting "show" was more popular than anything on television. And I never heard the sheriff criticized for his sense of humor.

Lenora Thurmond had no doubt heard such stories. This may have been a contributing factor to her being "emotionally unsuited" for residence in jail. Rita Schwerner obtained her immediate release by paying her fine of fifty dollars.

Mickey Schwerner was released on Wednesday, along with "the kids." He joked about the experience and told stories about bugs in the mattresses and a woeful shortage of toilet paper. He felt kindly toward his fellow prisoner who, he thought, had kept him from being hit. The truth is that every white prisoner had been ordered *not* to hit him. The same power which safeguarded Mickey in Meridian outside the jail had reached inside the jail and guarded him.

The men with the power in Meridian still wanted neither constitutional issues nor violence, in jail or out, in their "handling" of agitators. Their "defense" plan was simple and intelligent: "Let's just keep everything quiet as possible. Don't give the reporters or the federal agents any reason to come in here."

Mickey not only went free; he also scored his first victory. He and his pickets had been arrested, but his boycott was effective. The Negroes were "sticking together" and neglecting to trade at the variety store. The store manager surrendered. He bought peace with an agreement to hire the Negro woman who had been trained at the Community Center. Her wages were to be the same as those of the white employees, and she would stand behind a counter and be clearly visible.

On Wednesday afternoon, however, the day he was released, Mickey spent an hour at the Lauderdale County Courthouse. He waited for charges against him to be heard, but there was no hearing and the charges were dismissed.

While he waited there, he was observed by a young man about his own age. He looked about like Bart Floyd looked in his mid-twenties. Hard-eyed and hard-handed. I was told that he made this statement:

"In some way I'm gonna get my hands on that nigger-loving Jew sonofabitch. And when I do, he ain't never gonna see the sunrise again!"

Later a federal grand jury was to indict the young man who made that statement as one of the conspirators who murdered Mickey Schwerner, Andrew Goodman, and James Chaney.

FIVE

Day by day, throughout May and early June, the flames of race hate were fanned in Mississippi. The battle for the Civil Rights Bill in Congress was reported as though Satan was battling God. Every newspaper, every radio and television station, carried Ross Barnett's daily tirades:

"We are facing the most critical hour in the history of our nation. We must either submit to the unlawful demands of the pressure groups or stand up like men and tell them 'Never!'

"Mississippi has been made the special target of the Communists and the Mixers because Mississippi has given this nation and the world the shining example of successful segregation."

"We will never abandon our time-honored and workable patterns of race relations. We will never yield to the Mixers."

The word *Mixers* was coined and popularized as a synonym for Communists. It appeared almost daily on front pages in heads like this:

COURT RULINGS FAVOR
MIXERS, COMMUNISTS

A Mixer is not a Negro: it is assumed by these people that every Negro wants to mix. A Mixer is a white person who is willing to mix. So a Mixer is a Communist, an atheist, a nigger-lover who approves of "banning the Bible." There is a sexual connotation. A Mixer is an advocate of that old scare "mongrelization."

Mississippi was "imperiled" not only by what was happening in Congress but also by a "tidal wave" which was forming in the North to "engulf us." During the impending summer the state was to be "invaded" by "hundreds of Mixers"; "misguided students" were to come "flooding" into Mississippi for

65

no other purpose than to Mix—and Mix—and "flaunt their Mixing in the faces of decent white people."

How was this invasion to be turned back? What levee could resist such a flood? How was "all that Mississippi holds dear" to be safeguarded against the "tidal wave of Mixers?"

Not by legal means. Not even a Mixer needs a permit to cross the Mississippi state line. Mixing violates no law. Mixers cannot be arrested legally, and if arrested illegally they can soon be freed.

Even so routine a development as ending of the school term would add to Mississippi's "peril." It would release hundreds of "hopped-up young niggers" to go chasing about the streets in their FREEDOM NOW T-shirts, picketing and canvassing, holding mass meetings and distributing leaflets.

How could men like Bart Floyd and Joe Pritchett and the other emasculators of Edward Aaron "protect their children" from such "perilous attacks" by Mixers? If the law couldn't protect them, how could they "stand up like men and tell them: 'Never!' "?

Here is the answer.

The white-supremacy terrorists and their active supporters in Mississippi adopted a *Master Plan for Protection.* Included in this Master Plan were four Protective Plans, each plan successively more violent, with any or all plans to be "activated as necessary." The four Protective Plans were known as Plan One, Plan Two, Plan Three, and Plan Four.

Plan One, for meeting the "peril" and "protecting our children," was Cross-Burnings and Leaflets.

On a single night in May the terrorists burned at least one cross in every Mississippi county. They burned twelve crosses in Neshoba County, at the same time but in twelve different places. One cross was burned on the courthouse lawn and illuminated the sheriff's office. The Jackson press reported a leaflet which screamed:

THE BLACK SAVAGES THREATEN TO
TURN MISSISSIPPI INTO A CONGO!

Plan Two was Burning and Dynamiting.

By the end of 1964 at least forty churches had been burned and innumerable homes had been dynamited.

Plan Three was Whippings.

No one knows how many whippings have occurred. Many victims of whippings never report them because they have been warned "If you talk and we have to come back, we'll kill yuh."

Plan Four—Extermination.

During the second week in May 1964 a decision to activate Plan Four was reached by a group of terrorists in Mississippi. This activation was not to be "against a nigger" but
"against a Mixer." A Mixer, as I explained, is a white man.
And what Mixer was Plan Four to be activated against?

THE "JEW-BOY WITH THE BEARD AT MERIDIAN"

I could not ascertain how many echelons of authority
knew of this decision. But I am convinced that several men
elsewhere in Mississippi, outside Lauderdale and Neshoba
counties, knew of it.

The word was passed. Plan Four activated. The "Jew-boy
with the beard at Meridian." Plan Four is coming. Already
ordered and approved. The "Jew-boy with the beard at Meridian."

The decision or order contained one provision. The conspirators were not strong enough with the police in Meridian
and Lauderdale County to "activate safely" in that county. So
Plan Four was to be activated in a nearby county.

I am convinced that perhaps two hundred men in Mississippi knew, not later than May twentieth, that Mickey
Schwerner was likely to be murdered the first time the conspirators could lay hands on him outside Lauderdale County.

• • •

If Mickey Schwerner suspected that he had been marked for
such a distinction, there was nothing in his conduct to indicate it. He had his own plans for the summer. They were:

Plan One: "Stepped-up activity in Meridian, using the kids
who will be out of school us well as Summer Volunteers."

Plan Two: "Stepped-up activity in the outlying counties,
using Summer Volunteers to help us."

Here is Rita's report of June 6, 1964:

A great deal has happened since my last report. On Friday,
May 22nd, we started a selective buying campaign aimed at
the three five and ten cent stores here in Meridian. They are
Kress's, Newberry's and Woolworth's. We had previously attempted to negotiate with the store managers to no avail. We
had written letters to their national offices with no replies.
We are asking for sales jobs for Negroes and for desegregation of the lunch counters. On May 23rd one young man was
arrested for passing out leaflets. On Saturday, May 30th, 11
more people were arrested for "interfering with a man's business." The trials were to take place on June 3rd, but our at-

torney obtained a week's continuance. He is attempting to
have the cases removed to Federal Court on the grounds that
no one can obtain a fair civil rights trial in a state court in
Mississippi. The boycott appears to be fairly successful, but a
delegation of ministers who attempted once more to speak
with the managers this morning was rebuffed. Any further
discussion will now have to be initiated by the managers. If
there is no breakthrough this week, further direct action, perhaps in the form of a picket line, is planned for next
Saturday. . . .

The Community Center is functioning fairly well, with
children using the facilities in greater number now that
school is out. It has become a place to explain to people the
importance of the Movement and the part they can play in it.
We received a shipment of 200 new dresses, of different sizes
and materials, and we are distributing them to needy persons.
We still follow the procedure that all Lauderdale County residents over 21 must register to vote before they receive
clothing or other help from this Center. We explain that this
is a necessary step toward relieving the conditions which
make the distribution of clothing necessary. The number of
women receiving clothing and cloth has been reduced since
this procedure was adopted about a month ago. But we feel
that at least the people we are reaching are really attempting
to help themselves. . . .

Over and over we keep saying to them: We can't help you.
We can only help you to help yourselves. Unless you are
willing to work and to take risks, the Movement can't succeed. So the Movement depends on *you*. . . .

We have been holding mass meetings frequently, and we
have one scheduled for every night this coming week. . . .

We are being thrown out of our house on Monday. We
have been able to find housing for everyone but Mickey and
myself. The two of us are searching for an apartment, but
what is available the people are afraid to rent to us, and
what we could have is not empty. We have been receiving
large numbers of prank calls since the latest boycott started,
and these calls now reach Freedom House all night long. We
don't like to take the phone off the hook, but we have started
to do so when we must go to sleep. On Thursday our water
was turned off, and on Friday the gas and electricity. We
now have the water and gas back, but not the electricity. All
of this is annoying and takes time to straighten out, but is to
be expected. It should be added that the clerks in the different companies are not anxious to help us the moment
they realize who Mickey is. . . .

We are, as usual, in need of money. We have $125 tied up
in bond right now. Rent on the office and other bills are due.

That was Rita Schwerner's last report. A traveling representative of CORE, Marvin Rich, gave me this recollection:

The last time I saw Mickey Schwerner and James Chaney was on Thursday, June 7th. I was in Meridian to evaluate their work in the Community Center. . . .

I got into town about 7 P.M. and learned that a mass meeting was scheduled for 7:30, so I drove to the church. Mickey, Jim and Lenora Thurmond were sitting on the street curb eating their dinner of American cheese, white bread and a quart of orange drink. A number of cars driven by youths wearing T-shirts emblazoned "Freedom Now CORE" brought people to the meeting from the scattered Negro sections of Meridian. . . .

Mickey explained to me the nonstructured operation of the Community Center. They developed new programs in response to interest. He asked me to get him 600 layettes to give away to women who graduated from classes he was planning in prenatal care. He had a local midwife willing to volunteer to teach the classes. He also asked that we get modeling clay and paints, brushes and paper for his youngsters to use. . . .

Mickey insisted that we put James Chaney on the task force. Chaney had been spending full time. His mother had five children. But, most important, Chaney was competent. On this trip I made to Louisiana and to Jackson, Canton and Meridian, Mississippi, there were requests for additional staff from each community. Chaney was the only one hired.

When I learned that for more than a month before he was murdered Mickey Schwerner had been under death sentence, I wondered if at any time during this month he had felt discouraged and considered going back to New York. A few days of despair could have saved his life. Did he feel that he was accomplishing something? Was he achieving his personal goal?

"Mickey was human, intensely human," Rita told me. "But if there were days in which he felt discouraged, he never showed it. He had this wonderful conviction that every human being is essentially good—that every individual knows what is good for himself and, if given a fair chance, will eventually choose what is good. So Mickey, lacking a capacity to hate, also lacked the normal capacity to feel disappointed. He shrugged off every rebuff or insult as temporary and meaningless. He couldn't resent opposition because he thought he understood it.

"Our losing the house was a disappointment to both of us.

Perhaps more to me than to him. We had bought furniture and made curtains and tried to turn it into a real Freedom House which could give a lift to everybody who entered it. It was comfortable and had a modern bathroom. Moreover we had been there long enough so that we knew the children on the block. And children are so important to people in our position. They are the ones who are not afraid of us. After listening to hateful telephone calls all day, it was nice to sit on the porch with two or three children in the evening and laugh and tell fairy tales.

"The way we were forced out of the house was irritating. I think it would have been easier if the terrorists had come in the night and thrown us into the street. But the power structure was too smart to allow that. Instead we'd come home and find the water cut off. The clerk would say that there had been some mistake, that the water would be turned back on at once. Maybe three days later we'd find the water back on, but the lights were off, or the gas. Finally they cut everything off and we had to get out. And we had no place to go. After nearly five months in Meridian, the Negroes were more afraid to take us into their homes than they had been at first. We had virtually no white friends."

I asked: "What about Mr. Jones? He had rented your house in his own name. Wasn't he powerful enough to keep it for you?"

"I guess he wasn't," Rita said. "For the first time he seemed to be a little tense toward us. He is a proud man, and proud of his membership in NAACP. He also wanted us more militant COFO people to be in Meridian. But he wanted us . . . well, not to make too much trouble. He had connections with the power structure. He could call them and get some things done. But it seemed like they had agreed to let him have a little agitation in Meridian, but not enough to really disturb anything. When we began the boycotts and the kids started getting arrested, Mr. Jones felt the heat. They began calling and telling him that they expected him to 'control the Negro Community,' and I suppose he began to feel a little irritation toward us."

The upstairs apartment which Mickey and Rita managed to rent on June eighth was the dilapidated one I have described, next to the funeral home. It was a dreary place, with no bathing facilities, and while they lived there Mickey and Rita were watched more carefully by the police than at any time before. The police watched them because the police knew others were watching them. The police either knew of or suspected a plan to murder Mickey, and the men who control

Meridian were still determined that it wouldn't happen there.

I asked Rita if she could recall even one occasion on which Mickey seemed downcast or appeared to feel he wasn't accomplishing much.

"I suppose the day after the Democratic primary in Mississippi might have been such a time for him," Rita replied. "A Negro woman had run against Senator John Stennis, and for the Movement it was important that the Negro candidate receive the largest possible vote. But, of the seventeen hundred Negroes in Lauderdale County who were qualified to vote, only about three hundred bothered to vote for the Negro candidate. The others either didn't vote at all or they voted for Senator Stennis. That was a jolt to Mickey. But he wasn't really downcast. He accepted that, too, as a temporary situation."

One afternoon in East Brunswick, New Jersey, at the home of Mrs. Louise Saul, I talked with four teen-age Negro girls from Meridian who had known Mickey and Rita and who had supported the Movement. One of them was Sue Brown, the smart, pretty high school girl who had worked in the Community Center. All four, with the help of white people including Mrs. Saul, were then attending college in New Jersey. I asked the four to tell me about Mickey and Rita, and I asked them for their judgment as to what was being accomplished in the Community Center.

"Well, first," Sue Brown said, "you must understand what it was that Mickey had. More than any white person I have ever known he could put a colored person at ease. To a group of young Negroes he didn't seem like a preacher, or a do-gooder, or a social worker, or somebody who was out slumming, or a reporter who had come to learn about Negroes. Mickey just seemed like folks. He was the only white man I have ever known that you could associate with and forget he was white. He didn't talk down or up to you, he just talked to you. He made you feel like he was interested in you, not because you were a Negro, but because you were folks, too. He never pretended that he knew what was best for you. He hadn't come to Mississippi to *tell* Negroes. He was just there to remind Negroes that they were folks like everybody else, and that they should walk like folks, and talk like folks, and insist that they be treated like folks."

A second girl said: "I'd say he did good just by being Mickey Schwerner, by wearing his overalls and his sweat shirt, and by being there. He did good every time he met a young Negro simply by the effect he had on the young Negro. Just being around Mickey was enough to make any young Negro feel better about his life situation."

A third girl said: "There was nothing striking about the way Mickey looked. He had very blue eyes, and a sort of kind face with his beard. But he just made you feel hopeful. And you didn't feel hopeful so much for Negroes as for the whole human race. You didn't feel sorry for yourself any more. If you felt sorry, you felt sorry for the whole human race."

"What about Rita?" I asked.

"Rita was different," Sue Brown said. "She was friendly, but not like Mickey. She was more impatient; she likes to finish what she starts. I got the impression that she was in Mississippi because Mickey wanted to be there."

Another girl said: "I think Rita liked the idea of liking people, but she just didn't like everybody."

The fourth girl said: "I think Rita would have gone back to New York if it had been left up to her. But Mickey didn't want to go back. By the time they killed him I think Mickey felt he belonged in Mississippi. I guess that's why they decided to kill him."

I then said to the four girls: "What I'm trying to understand is the size of Mickey Schwerner's accomplishment. He was being supported in Mississippi by people up North who expected him to accomplish something. He and two other young men lost their lives. Was the accomplishment worth the price? Grant that Mickey was a good man. Was he effectively good? Nehru once said: 'It isn't enough for one to be good; one must be effectively good.' Give me some idea of the magnitude of Mickey's accomplishment among the Negroes of Mississippi."

The four girls reflected for a moment. Then Sue Brown said: "If you put it that way, maybe Mickey wasn't accomplishing very much. A preacher like Billy Graham can tell what he's accomplishing by the number of souls he is saving. If Mickey was sent to Mississippi to save white souls, he failed completely. I don't know of a single soul he saved. If he was in Mississippi to enlist Negroes in the Movement . . . well, he did enlist a few. We attracted a good many young kids to the Center. But most of them came to play ping-pong. We attracted women to the Center when we had something to give them. Most of the people at the mass meetings came out of curiosity. Certainly, in the six months he lived in Mississippi, Mickey didn't get many new voters. Maybe he got one woman a better job. I don't think he changed the attitude of a single white person. All he really did was encourage a few teen-age Negroes. And maybe he persuaded as many as a hundred older Negroes to take some risks and try to qualify to vote."

"He did more than that," a second girl said. "Maybe he didn't do much in quantity—like the preacher saving a lot of souls. But he did good just by being down there. It made a lot of Negroes feel better just to know that there was a white man in the world like Mickey."

During the last week in May Mickey was visited by his friend Ed Pitt, the tall Negro social worker from Hamilton-Madison House.

"I wanted to see how Mickey was making it," Pitt told me. "I had never doubted that he could make it. I found that he had changed a lot in five months. He was more mature; he had his feet on the ground; he had found himself. I'd describe him as of that date as a pacifist, a humanist, a young man at peace with himself and completely dedicated to trying to help build a peaceful world."

"I belong right here in Mississippi, Ed," Mickey Schwerner had said to Ed Pitt. "Nothing threatens peace among men like the idea of white supremacy. Nowhere in the world is the idea of white supremacy more firmly entrenched, or more cancerous, than in Mississippi. The Ku Klux are as much the victims of white supremacy as the Negroes are. So this is the decisive battleground for America: and every young American who wants to have a part in the decision should be here."

. . .

Ironically, while the conspirators watched and waited to catch him in an "outlying" county, Mickey Schwerner was anxious to expand his activities in those very counties. The conspirators wanted to catch him in Kemper or Neshoba or Clarke county, and he, unsuspecting, wanted to give them their chance.

"There was a good reason why Mickey wanted to do more in the outlying counties," Rita explained. "The Negroes in Meridian were *relatively* well off. They suffered from a minimum of police brutality. They were not herded into a ghetto. About seventeen hundred of them voted. The schools, though much inferior to the national average and segregated, were better than elsewhere in Mississippi. Many Negroes lived comfortably. Therefore most of them, particularly the adults, were unwilling to take risks. They pointed to what they had, and they wanted to wait or go slow. So in Meridian our support was chiefly teen-agers. But in the outlying counties life was much harder for Negroes, they had less to lose, so the adults were ready to take more risks. It was this interest of adult Negroes in pushing for immediate gains that attracted Mickey to Neshoba and other outlying counties."

"It's always that way with subject people," Pitt explained. "The heavier their burdens, the more willing they are to risk death for freedom. When Mickey called on adults in Lauderdale County, they often told him they were busy, to come back tomorrow. But when he went to Neshoba County he found Negro adults ready to talk, and to listen to him, even in defiance of the sheriff and the Ku Klux."

As early as February Mickey had begun making trips into the other counties. His reports contain several references:

> On Thursday Matt Suarez and myself went into Newton County to talk about the Freedom Registration campaign. We contacted two men and were told that there is to be a meeting of the Newton County NAACP on Sunday, Feb. 23rd. We are invited to attend. At this meeting we expect to lay the foundation for the Freedom registration project in Newton County. . . .
>
> This week we were glad to receive a visit from five men from Preston, Kemper County, who came down for instruction. They are interested not only in voter registration but also in the Federal programs that are available to farmers and businessmen. They have agreed to obtain a meeting place for registration classes in or around Preston which could serve northern Kemper and southern Winston counties. . . .
>
> This week we attended a meeting in Clarke County to organize a voter registration committee. We met at the Little Zion Church outside of Stonewall. Because of the shifts in the factory at Stonewall, we held two meetings. In all about 32 local men and women attended; and after Matt Suarez and I explained the various programs and why they are so important, there was a fair amount of enthusiasm.

In March, after James Chaney returned from Canton and began working full-time at the Meridian Community Center, Mickey Schwerner began using Chaney to scout outlying counties. A car belonging to CORE had been turned over to the Meridian Center. It was a blue Ford station wagon with a Hinds County (Jackson) license plate. The car had been used by several COFO workers in Jackson, Canton, Carthage, and other trouble spots, and it was known to the terrorists and to the sheriffs and highway patrolmen. A picture of it, with its license number, had been circulated, and many were "on the lookout for it."

Despite the fact that the car was marked, Chaney used it effectively. in "spying out" rural Negro groups which might be persuaded to "sign up to try to vote." He had advantages over Schwerner and even over other Negroes. In several ways he could be inconspicuous. Not only was he a Negro but, more important, he was not an intellectual; he wore no beard; his speech was "like a nigger's ought to be"; so he appeared ordinary. He was of average height, and he knew how to move among white men without attracting attention.

Lauderdale County is in east Mississippi: its eastern boundary is the Alabama state line. North of Lauderdale is Kemper County, also on the Alabama line. Kemper has long been known as "Bloody Kemper," because "it's so easy to get killed over there." West of Kemper is Neshoba County. Neshoba, Kemper, and Lauderdale have a common corner. Philadelphia, county seat of Neshoba, is thirty-six miles northwest of Meridian, and the road runs across the common corner.

In April Chaney made his first trips into Neshoba. Schwerner accompanied him twice, and they went into Philadelphia and met several Negroes. They knew Neshoba was a maximum-danger county. They knew it was one of the counties where the sheriff had been elected on the promise that he'd "handle the niggers and the outsiders." They knew the sheriff and his only deputy had friends who were Ku Klux types. They knew that if they were arrested in Neshoba, one way or another they might find themselves in terrorist hands. Therefore every trip that they, or any other COFO worker, made into Neshoba was a game of hide-and-seek or cops-and-robbers: like Americans sneaking into Nazi-occupied France to contact the Resistance.

Witnesses at the trial testified that both Neshoba County Sheriff Lawrence Rainey and his only deputy, Cecil Price, were members of the White Knights of the Ku Klux Klan. In addition, the man who preceded Rainey as sheriff and who, in 1967, was elected to succeed Rainey, Ethel Glen (Hop) Barnette, was identified as a Klansman. All three were among the eighteen defendants at the trial.

During the last week in May, Ed Pitt, while visiting Meridian, made a "night run" into rural Neshoba County with Chaney. He recalled it for me:

"Chaney had been negotiating with several Negroes in the Longdale farming community. He was trying to persuade them to risk allowing a Freedom School to be conducted in the Mount Zion Methodist Church. He had urged them to allow Schwerner to speak at the church the following Sunday. We went up there to get their final answer.

"We left Meridian about dusk, so it was dark when we hit the Neshoba line. Chaney turned off the main road and began speeding along narrow, red-clay, back-country roads. He seemed to know the terrain like the back of his hand. And, man, he *flew*! I mean he drove seventy and eighty miles an hour on back roads. Sometimes he'd cut down to his parking lights, like I've seen in war pictures, with guys speeding through blackouts. Chaney was a good driver, and he had a great sense of direction. He said to me: 'I sure feel sorry for any living thing that steps in front of us tonight. Because, man, we can't afford to stop for nothing!'

"As we drove I was struck by the fact that we couldn't see a light anywhere. Every now and then we'd pass a shanty that I'd guess was occupied, but it was dark as pitch. 'They don't show no lights now,' Chaney said. 'If you're a Negro in this county and the boss man thinks you might be thinking about trying to qualify to vote, man you black out when night comes. You sure don't want to attract any attention.' I asked Chaney how we were going to recognize the house we were coming to visit. 'We'll find it,' he replied. 'We better find the right one. We pull up to the wrong one, and you may never see your wife and kid again.'

"I'll never forget our visit to that house. I didn't see the house at first, or even the little road going into it. When Chaney pulled in there I thought the place was deserted. But he cut the engine and we got out. Then he whistled two or three times, and I saw a crack of light. Honest, it was just like war! Those people were afraid for themselves, and they were even more afraid for us. They kept cautioning us about what roads to avoid and what road to take. They wanted to talk to us, but they also wanted us to hurry and get out. When I gave the woman a handful of leaflets about voter instruction, you'd have thought she was handling TNT. She took them and hid them. Then they told us that there had been a meeting with a lot of head-shaking, but they had decided to let Schwerner speak on Sunday morning, May thirty-first. The man said: 'God help us, it may be our last act on this earth. But I guess if a man don't try to vote today he ain't *nothing!*'

"We left that house like the Israelites spying out Canaan. Chaney drove even faster, with less light, and I thought every curve might be our last one. When we hit the Lauderdale County line he switched on the headlights, slowed down, and breathed easy."

Ed Pitt told me that story in a New York hotel suite. When he finished I said: "You know, as well as I, that not a dozen Negroes in that poor little community will ever vote. You know that most of the young Negroes from Longdale have already gone North, and the kids are only waiting to finish high school to go. You know that there are only two thousand Negroes in Neshoba County, and if all of them voted they'd still be outvoted eight to one. So why would a man like you go chasing around in Neshoba County on such a cops-and-robbers wild-goose chase?"

"That's a good question," he said. "My wife will love you for asking it. Because, of course, she asked it. And you know the answer as well as I do. The power of an idea . . . the idea that a poor Negro farmer in Mississippi has the right to cast a ballot. That's a dangerous, revolutionary idea. Men will risk death to promote it. They'll go on wild-goose chases and play cops-and-robbers. Other men will commit murder to defeat it. They'll meet in the dark, and lie in wait, and they'll cut and burn, whip and kill. You know what an idea'll do."

"Yeah, I guess that's it," I said. "And each side feeds on the other. They both find exhilaration in the conflict and intrigue."

On Sunday morning, May 31, Decoration Day week end, Chaney and Schwerner went back to Longdale. About forty people were present in the small, weather-beaten church. It stands two miles off the pavement, down a narrow, red-clay road. Schwerner spoke feelingly about the idea of One Man, One Vote.

"Former Governor Barnett," he said, "says that now is the time for white men to stand up like men and say to you 'Never!' I say that now is the time for Negroes in Mississippi to stand up like men and say to Barnett 'Now!' You have been slaves too long. We can help you help yourselves. Let us hold a Freedom School in this church. Meet us here, and we'll train you so you can qualify to vote. Then you can march into Philadelphia, and the sheriff and all the Ku Klux can't keep you from walking in your courthouse and writing your name on the poll list. Because the Government of the United States must be walking right there beside you."

After listening to Mickey Schwerner, the Negroes in the Mount Zion Church at Longdale did what he asked. They voted for the Freedom School. So before dawn on Tuesday, June 16, the Ford station wagon slipped out of Meridian and headed for Oxford, Ohio, where three hundred summer volunteers were training to come to Mississippi. Mickey and Rita were in the station wagon. They took it instead of the Volkswagen so they could bring back more volunteers. They were going to Oxford to assist in the training. They also intended to select one particular superior and dedicated volunteer whose job would be to work with Chaney in the Freedom School at Longdale and elsewhere in Neshoba County.

SIX

To begin understanding a people one must first try to see them as they see themselves. Here is how Philadelphia and Neshoba County, Mississippi, describe themselves in their Chamber of Commerce literature:

> Located in the East Central part of the beautiful Magnolia State . . . Neshoba County is a thriving community of over 21,000 people. The county seat is Philadelphia, which has a population of 6,000. The county is approximately 24 miles square . . . with a land area of over 269,000 acres.
>
> The most outstanding attraction . . . is the friendly and hospitable people who make the area their home. A visitor to our community finds an old-fashioned welcome and a degree of friendliness that exists in no other place.
>
> YOU'LL LOVE PHILADELPHIA AND NESHOBA COUNTY
> The city is particularly attractive for new industry, with an abundant supply of raw materials, abundant labor, low cost of living, low tax rate, and the wonderful friendliness of the area. . . .
>
> THE HEART OF THE CHOCTAW NATION
> . . . The government established an Indian agency here in 1918. In the vicinity of Philadelphia are seven federally operated day schools which educate the Choctaw Indian children.
>
> Each year at the Pearl River Indian School (just outside of Philadelphia) the Choctaw Indians hold their annual Fair. . . . They display their arts and crafts and hold a series of stickball games under the ancient rules of their ancestors. . . . Also during this festival, the Choctaw Indian Princess is selected to rule over the Choctaw Indian Nation during the coming year.
>
> The Choctaw Indian has adopted most of the ways of the white man, but he is still Choctaw in language and dress.

78

Most depend on agriculture for income, however, more and more Choctaws are engaging in skilled and semi-skilled work each year.

Industry in the area is diversified. The Pet Milk Company operates a large receiving station in Philadelphia which buys $2,000,000 worth of raw milk annually. The Wells-Lamont Corporation has one of their larger glove manufacturing operations in the city. Over 25,000,000 pairs of gloves are made annually. U.S. Electrical Motors, Inc. [a division of Emerson Electric Company] makes industrial motors in Philadelphia.

The lumber industry brings over $3,500,000 annually into the county. Philadelphia has three mills: the A. DeWeese Lumber Company, the Molpus Lumber Company, and the Deemer Lumber Company. Each year these companies produce 50,000,000 board feet of lumber, 90% of which is pine. About 56% of the county's land is planted in pine timber. Richton Tie and Timber Company operates a pulpwood receiving station in the area.

Beef and dairy cattle are speedily bringing about an agricultural balance with cotton. . . . Corn . . . remains a major crop.

. . . The two electric companies furnish low-cost TVA and REA powers.

. . . Taxes in the county fall far below the national average.

[Some typical average wage rates: Electrician $1.92 per hour; Welder $1.83; Machinist $1.70; Sewing machine operator $1.32; Truck driver $1.43; Bookkeeper, male $1.87, female $1.25; all unskilled jobs, $1.25.]

There are 15 churches in Philadelphia [14 Protestant and one Catholic.] There is a new 80-bed Hill-Burton hospital. There is a swimming pool and a nine-hole golf course. Numerous lakes and ponds offer fine year-around fishing, and for the hunter Neshoba County is a paradise.

[Percentage of home ownership: 80%. Average monthly rental: 2-bedroom house $40; 3-bedroom house $50. Average purchase price: 2-bedroom $10,000; 3-bedroom $12,000.]

The nationally known Neshoba County Fair takes place every summer on the largest camp ground of its kind in the nation. A full week of fun and fellowship provide the setting for this unique fair.

Meaningful sayings in Neshoba County are "Niggers are moving North, Yankees are moving South." "Cotton is moving West, cattle are moving East." And "We're swapping niggers for Yankees, and it's the best swap we could make."

There has been an exodus. Twenty years ago the population of the county, including Philadelphia, was twenty-eight thousand. Philadelphia had five thousand. Now Philadelphia has six thousand and the entire county has twenty thousand. So the crossroads communities and the countryside have lost nine thousand inhabitants. This has caused the countryside to look vacant. You see no large cotton or corn fields—only pine trees and pastures, with swamps and lakes, and ponds created to cool and water the herds.

Much of the population loss has been Negroes going to Chicago, Detroit, and Los Angeles. Some of the loss has been the superior young whites, particularly the college graduates, seeking larger opportunity and cultural advantage. As always, most of the emigrants have been between eighteen and forty-five, the dissatisfied and the ambitious, so that a high percentage of the remaining two thousand Negroes are old and on relief and are therefore resented. Half of the Negroes live in "niggertowns" in Philadelphia; the other half live in several rural pockets off the main roads, where the Negroes own small parcels of land. They "scratch out a little cotton" and exist with the aid of the relief checks and often with gifts sent from the North.

No area in America has benefited more from federal aid. The TVA and the REA; farm price supports, the soil bank, FHA, even the federal bonus which each cattle-raiser collects for building a pond; the Hill-Burton hospital; the federal contributions to old-age assistance—all have helped make Neshoba County a better place to live.

And it is a good place to live—if you are white and have a job and want simplicity. Most people who move there from the North like it. There is no traffic problem. Housing is cheap. Neither the air nor the streams are polluted. The hunting is excellent. Fish bite the year round. Taxes are low. Weather is kind. Television reception is good. Competition is relaxed. Nobody is in a hurry. So if you are white and Christian and not a union organizer or a civil rights advocate, you may agree that Neshoba County is the friendliest place on earth.

Even if you are a Negro you may find it friendly—if you'll stay in your place. If you'll "talk like a nigger" and "act like a nigger." If you'll call all white men Mister. If you'll report for work on time, "work like a nigger" at your menial job, then get out of sight. But don't try to register to vote. Or use the public swimming pool or public golf course. Don't educate your son and try to get him a job as a fireman or a policeman. Don't educate your daughter and try to get her a job as a salesgirl or as a secretary at the courthouse. If you do something like that you'll reveal that you are an "agitator," and you better take the next bus to Chicago. You aren't being friendly. You are trying to make trouble and give the friendly community a bad image.

"Proof" that they are right is always available to the people of Neshoba County. Every year a few Negroes come back from Chicago and report how glad they are to get back. Life was "a lot tougher up there." Rent was "high as a cat's back." The winter was "cold as kraut." And "folks yah met on the street just didn't care whether yah lived or died."

On Tuesday, June 16, 1964, virtually every white person in Neshoba County believed that he lived in a "law-abiding, friendly community." He didn't believe Neshoba County had any race trouble "to speak of." Race trouble was a terror that existed in New York and Washington, where the streets were unsafe, and where Negro gangs roamed the parks looking for white victims. Race trouble was the work of "atheists" and "Communists" and political opportunists. Race trouble was the result of unconstitutional decisions by a "Communist-and-atheist-influenced" U.S. Supreme Court.

In the conflict over civil rights the people of Neshoba County never doubted that they were right. They saw themselves libeled, misrepresented, and unjustly attacked by the national press and television, and by assorted "atheists, Communists, misguided do-gooders, Jews, and nigger-lovers." A good, friendly way of life was under attack from an evil, unfriendly way of life. The people of Neshoba County could imagine nothing more ridiculous or uncalled-for than an atheist-Jewish social worker from "Harlem" coming to Mississippi to try to solve the "race problem."

"The problem is in New York," they said, "not in Neshoba County. Here life is peaceful, safe, and friendly. Up there no man dares venture into the streets at night. The parks are dangerous in broad daylight. So any man who comes here from New York saying he wants to solve the race problem is at best a hypocrite and a fool. At worst he is a Communist, an atheist, and an enemy of the United States. We hope he gets out alive: we don't hold with murder. But if he gets hurt, it's his own fault. He came looking for trouble and found it. He should have stayed where he belonged."

• • •

If you were white and not a union organizer or a civil rights worker, or an outside reporter or photographer, one of the friendliest men in friendly Neshoba County on June 16, 1964, was the sheriff, Lawrence A. Rainey. He had a grin, a wave, and a good word for every friend he met.

In truth, when I met the sheriff in the early days of the search, he was not unfriendly. He gave me a pad to make notes on and answered my questions courteously. I began life as a police reporter, and under different circumstances I can imagine the sheriff and me enjoying a joke together. He was forty-one, six foot two, and weighed 240. He looked meaty, barrel-chested, and in his jaw was a chew of Red Man tobacco the size of a golf ball. He wore a khaki uniform with calf-length boots and a khaki cattleman's hat turned up on the sides. His belt bulged with polished leather, burnished brass and lead ammunition, and a heavy holstered gun. He drove a new tan Oldsmobile with a powerful red light on top, and in the car were guns, nightsticks, and extra cartons of Red Man.

The sheriff was born on a farm in adjoining Kemper County. With limited education, he learned to be an automobile mechanic, and he worked as a mechanic in Canton. A kidney ailment is said to have kept him out of military service. In 1957 he became a Canton city policeman, and in 1959 he killed his first Negro. "A Chicago nigger," the sheriff explained to me. "He had me down choking me." He then moved to Philadelphia and worked on the city police force. In 1961 he became a sheriff's deputy. He killed a second Negro. "A crazy nigger," the sheriff said. "We were taking him to the state hospital. He grabbed a gun out of the glove compartment, and I killed him in an exchange of gunfire." In 1963 he was elected sheriff on his promise to "handle the niggers and the outsiders," and in January 1964 he assumed office.

Sheriff Rainey lives in a modest home with his wife and two sons, eight and ten. He emphasized to me that he was a *Southern* Methodist.

The only deputy, Cecil Price, was a younger and somewhat less formidable copy of the sheriff. Only twenty-seven, he came to Philadelphia from Madison County (Canton) when he was nineteen, as a salesman for dairy supplies. For five years he traveled every back road in Neshoba County, calling on dairymen. He then became fire chief of Philadelphia at a time when the city hired two full-time firemen. For two years he also served as a week-end policeman, handling ball games and dances. He became a father for the first time in October 1964 with the birth of a son.

When Rainey became sheriff, Price was his choice for deputy.

A sheriff and his deputy are particularly close in Mississippi because neither is salaried. The sheriff works on a complicated and lucrative fee system (he is also tax collector) and he himself hires, fires, and pays his deputy.

To me Price seemed to lack Rainey's friendliness. Rainey was the big, gruff, unlettered countryman, deadly on occasion but capable of relaxed laughter. Price seemed tight-lipped, ambitious, suspicious of everybody. Were I a Negro or a civil rights worker, I'd hate to meet either of them in an alley, in a jail cell, or along a back road. But I had rather take my chances with Rainey.

In a town the size of Philadelphia, where the business area fills less than eight square blocks, a uniformed man the size of Sheriff Rainey casts a long shadow. He and his deputy are the most visible citizens in town. The center block is the courthouse; the sheriff's office is the front office in the courthouse; and the sheriff's two reserved parking places are in the center of the courthouse block. Present or missing, his car attracts attention. A block away in one direction is the city hall and police station. A block away in another direction is the Hotel Benwalt, where the Rotary Club meets. Between the hotel and the city hall is the jail, frequently visited by the sheriff and his deputy. And a block from the sheriff's office in a third direction is the weekly newspaper, the Neshoba *Democrat*. Spaced among all these landmarks are barber shops, beauty shops, drugstores, and variety stores.

So the movements of the sheriff and his deputy are noted and discussed every hour of every business day; like Matt Dillon's on *Gunsmoke*.

A third, but not usually uniformed, law-enforcement figure at the courthouse is Justice of the Peace Leonard Warren. His office is in the courthouse, and most miscreants are brought before him. He attracts attention by being the physical opposite of Rainey and Price: skinny, no more than 140 pounds, chicken-necked, with a prominent Adam's apple. He, too, likes to don the cattleman's hat, the gun, and the nightstick and work as a part-time cop.

In addition to Rainey, Price, and Warren, the law is served in Philadelphia by six city policemen, two of whom are always on duty. Two state highway patrolmen, Earl R. Poe and Harry J. Wiggs, live in Philadelphia, are stationed there, and report by radio to the Meridian substation. Poe and Wiggs are usually within a few miles of Philadelphia. A third highway patrolman, Inspector M. R. King, is also based in Philadelphia. There is a volunteer auxiliary police organization and a National Guard unit. These are "lily-white Southern Gentlemen," sworn to preserve the Mississippi way of life.

Some of these men, in June 1964, were members of the

Ku Klux Klan; others had family, business, social, or political connections with Klansmen.

Canton, like Philadelphia, is on east-west State Highway 16. Canton is fifty-five miles due west of Philadelphia, and Canton became a center of race trouble in January 1964. Both Rainey and Price had once lived in Canton, and Rainey had been a policeman there. So both of them had been briefed by Canton officers on what and whom "to look out for."

In April they began hearing about Mickey Schwerner's work in Meridian; when Schwerner and Chaney made their first trips into Neshoba County Rainey and Price were informed. They had the picture of the Ford station wagon, which had been used at Canton, and they had both white and Negro informers. Subsequently they both observed the station wagon, and they were informed of Schwerner's speech at Longdale on May 31.

Between Monday, June 1, and Tuesday, June 16, Negroes in the Longdale community told me they saw the sheriff's car cruising along the red clay road past the Mount Zion Methodist Church at least three times. The sheriff obviously knew that the Negroes were planning to hold a Freedom School at the church.

Did the sheriff also know the plan to kill Schwerner? Did he know that some of the Lauderdale and Neshoba County white-supremacy terrorists had "got together" and that they were planning to "activate Plan Four" in a joint operation? Did he know that these terrorists already had selected a burial site for Schwerner, "a place no damn federal agent would ever think of?" Did he know that they had set Tuesday, June 16, as the night they would "grab the Jew-boy with the beard and exterminate him?"

There was method in the selection of June 16 for murder. The State Democratic Party had set June 16 as the date for precinct meetings. As part of its political-education program COFO was urging all registered Negro voters, together with those who were trying to register, to try to attend the precinct meetings and try to help select delegates to the county conventions. It was correctly assumed that the Negroes would not be allowed to participate in the State Democratic Party meetings, and it was planned that the Negroes, with their white allies, calling themselves the Freedom Democratic Party, would then hold their own precinct meetings and ultimately challenge the white supremacists at the Democratic National Convention. So those who were planning the murder expected June 16 to be a day of trouble. In addition, the summer "invasion" of Mississippi by college students was to begin on June 22. The terrorists reasoned that the disappearance of Schwerner on the night following the precinct meetings would be doubly effective. It would "scare niggers who are thinking about voting," and it would scare the "Commie college students who are thinking about coming to Mississippi."

It was the group in Lauderdale County who somehow decided that Schwerner would be at the Longdale church on Tuesday evening, June 16. Those in Meridian notified the people in Neshoba County and the joint operation was "laid on."

This, of course, was a mistake by the Meridian group. How was it made? Several of them are veterans, and they take pride in their intelligence. They boast that they have infiltrated "everything" in Lauderdale County and that they can learn "anything they want to know." How then did they decide that Schwerner would be at Longdale at 10 P.M. on June 16, when in fact he would be in Oxford, Ohio? I tried to learn how this mistake was made, but never found a believable explanation.

On June 16 the regular Democratic Party held its precinct meetings throughout Mississippi. Negroes were not allowed to participate and no Neshoba County Negroes attempted to attend. The planned meetings of the Freedom Democratic Party were postponed when Negroes received word that informers had tipped off the sheriff of the meeting places. But Tuesday night was the regular meeting night for the "leaders and stewards" of the Mount Zion Methodist Church at Longdale. Darkness comes late on June 16: it is an exceptionally long-working day in cotton patches. So it was close to 9 P.M. when four automobiles—two sedans and two pickups— parked under the trees at the church, and seven men and three women went inside, turned on the lights, and began their regular business meeting.

One old Negro farmer explained to me: "You see, us Methodists don't pay the preacher any more on Sunday. The Baptists still do. But us Methodists we don't mention money any more on Sunday. We waits and comes back on Tuesday night to get up the preacher's money. And that's what we were doing."

About 10 P.M. the meeting broke up, and the ten Methodists started to leave the church. But outside they found a military demonstration. Perhaps as many as thirty men were lined up precisely, with rifles and shotguns. Other men were at the back of the church. The ten Negroes were allowed to reach their cars and pull out into the dirt road. Two of the cars turned north; the other two turned south. Then the white men began shouting, to one another and to the Negroes, and both pairs of Negro cars were stopped by other cars blocking the road. The Negro cars going south had proceeded about a hundred yards; so had the two cars going north. This placed the two groups of Negroes about two hundred yards apart, and each group had been intercepted by white men. What had happened? Why had the white men allowed the Negroes to leave the churchyard, then quickly intercepted them on the narrow road?

Here is the explanation. This was the first joint operation of the Meridian and Neshoba County groups who were trying to activate Plan Four. The Meridian men were holding the road south of the church; the Neshoba men were north of the church. A mixed group had confronted the Negroes and let them pass because the conspirators wanted only Schwerner and thought he was still in the church. When they didn't find him, they shouted to the others to hold the Negroes and search their cars to see if Schwerner was hiding in one of them.

All the Negroes were forced to cut off their lights and get out of their cars while the white men searched and questioned. Where the hell was the "Jew-boy with the beard?"

"Wasn't that a Freedom Meeting they were holding?" When both groups realized their mistake, each reacted differently. The north or Neshoba group allowed the Negroes to leave unharmed. But the south or Meridian group had traveled farther and had been drinking more. So they "took it out on the niggers." They beat them all, broke one woman's collarbone before they let them drive away.

Then the two groups congregated back at the churchyard. They were all mad. The Meridian group were blaming each other for the misinformation; the Neshoba group were cussing the Meridian group for "bringing us out here on a snipe hunt." They were all worried that Schwerner might learn they were "laying for him" and might either leave Mississippi or quit coming into Neshoba County. The Neshoba group denounced the Meridian group for beating the four Negroes, saying it might reach the papers where Schwerner would see it.

The row lasted more than an hour. At one point it became so fierce that gunfire was imminent. Several guns were drawn, and had a match been struck at the right instant the cause of mankind might have been served by a shootout. Finally they all agreed that one way or another they'd get "the goddam

Jew anyway." The Neshoba group withdrew, leaving the Meridian group still drinking in the churchyard. Rain was threatening. As the Meridian group started to leave, several of them noticed that someone had brought ten gallons of Diesel fuel, perhaps with which to burn Schwerner's Ford station wagon.

Rather than haul the fuel back to Meridian, someone poured it inside the church, struck a match, and left the church in flames.

Klansmen involved in the murder were alarmed when I published this account of Klan activities on the night of June 16th. How had I learned of the joint activity of the Lauderdale and Neshoba groups? How had I learned that the Lauderdale Klansmen, south of the church, were the ones who beat up the Negroes? Who told me of the drinking? Of the disagreements between the two factions?

I also seem to have been wrong in reporting that the Klansmen expecting to catch Schwerner and murder him on June 16th. My information had led me to believe that the Lauderdale Klansmen, before they left Meridian, knew of the meeting to be held at the Longdale church. This seems to have been inaccurate.

Delmar Dennis testified that he, with other members of the Lauderdale group, met with the Neshoba group during the evening of June 16th "in an abandoned gym in Neshoba County." He said that "Killen opened the meeting but Hop Barnette interrupted and said that on his way over to the meeting he passed Mt. Zion Church [Longdale] and a meeting was being held." Dennis quoted Barnette as saying: "It must be an important meeting because it was heavily guarded." Dennis said the group decided to send "volunteers" to the church. Dennis said that Wayne Roberts, Hop Barnette and Billy Wayne Posey left for the church, all of them armed.

Dennis said Billy Birdsong returned (to the abandoned gym) and gave a report "that the group from Meridian was guarding one of the exits of the church and that all the Negroes who left by that exit were being beaten."

Dennis said that when he and other members of the Lauderdale group left Neshoba County for Meridian "Wayne Roberts had blood on him, his knuckles were bloody, and he told me he got this when he was beating a Negro."

Another Klansman who was an FBI informer was Meridian Police Sergeant Wallace Miller. He testified that Killen told him that "they burned the church to get the civil rights worker up there, and he was referring to Schwerner."

So apparently I was wrong in reporting that the Klansmen thought they would catch Schwerner on June 16th.

. . .

One of the many tragic ironies in this story is that such an act of barbarism should have fallen on Longdale. It must be one of the least offensive communities on earth. There is nothing to it: an abandoned school, two old Negro grave-yards (Baptist and Methodist), and a few isolated shacks along a dirt road. It lies off Highway 16, eight miles due east of Philadelphia. In it there is no conflict between whites and Negroes because there are no whites. The farmland is too poor to attract whites. There are only poor Negro farmers, owning a little land, "scratching it out" with the help of those gifts from up North and those relief checks.

It's an area for walking. The trees meet over the narrow road, and the only sounds you hear, once the little cotton patches are laid by, are birds and woodcutters, and an old man singing "You're as Welcome as the Flowers in May."

Eight days after the church burning and three days after the disappearance I was told: "We don't bother no white folks and usually they don't pay no attention to us. We just live here and scratches it out. The children go into town on the bus to school, and when they get big enough they go off to the Army and to Chicago. The old folks stays here, and a few of the young ones comes back when the old folks get down in bed and has to have help until they get up there in the churchyard."

There was shock and resignation. "Well," a woman said, "when the young white man come and asked to be heard, I was scared but I was for letting him speak. So he spoke and we listened. About forty of us. The young white man said we was slaves as long as we couldn't vote, and he said a lot of young white folks was coming here to help us vote. He said he wanted to hold a Freedom School in the church so all the young folks could teach us to vote.

"Well, some of us was afraid, but some of us thought the time had come to stand up and ask the white man for our rights. I guess the word got out that we was going to have a Freedom School. Now our church is gone and two young white men and a young Negro man are gone. They are dead and lying in some river or swamp or unmarked grave. For their sake we should have known better than let 'em come in here."

An old man summed up: "Yessir, a lot o' gentlemen have been out here to see us this week, and the tough white man has let us alone. We haven't been threatened one time since all you visitors came. But we know how it'll be. As soon as all you gentlemen are gone, then the tough white man will come back and he'll say:

" 'Now you niggers get back in your place. We don't want to hear nothing else out of you. And if you make any trouble, or talk to any federal men, we'll put you in the river just like we done the other three.'

"That's the way it goes. It's safe for us to talk while all you visitors are around. But when you leave, then it gets mighty lonesome out here. There ain't nobody under these pine trees except us and the big man with guns buckled on and the red light flashing on top of his big car. Things will quiet down and things will be just like they was. The young ones will grow up and go to Chicago, and the old ones will stay here and plant and pick our cotton and die and be buried at home."

I suspect only an agrarian can understand the Negroes of Longdale. They love the land. They are like desert Indians. They don't want to go to Chicago; they are willing to pay the Mississippi price for a place to belong. They value an old churchyard, an old gravestone with a sentimental inscription, and a Mama and Papa to be buried next to, and to stand with on That Great Gittin' Up Mawnin'.

Movements are for the young and the crowded. Not for old folks dying around old churchyards. For all my sympathy for Mickey Schwerner, I wish he hadn't led those terrorists to Longdale.

. . .

Mickey Schwerner and James Chaney spent three days at Oxford, Ohio, where college students who had volunteered for a summer's work in Mississippi were trained for a week on the campus of the Western College for Women. The National Council of Churches paid training expenses for the group.

Mickey and Rita Schwerner, as well as James Chaney, took part in the widely publicized training program. The students were told:

That they were not to lead or take part in demonstrations but were only to live with Negro families and try to help the Negroes qualify to vote.

That they were to work with school-age Negroes and pre-school-age Negroes and to try to help them close the educational gap between themselves and the whites.

That they were to try to help Negroes of all ages to qualify for better jobs.

That, by living with Negroes, they were to demonstrate that they did not regard Negroes as Untouchables, or as socially inferior beings, and that Negroes should be admitted to all public places and to all forms of public activity.

That they should expect taunts, verbal abuse, blows, arrests, and jail terms, but that they should respond only and always in a nonviolent manner.

"It was like another holiday for us," Rita told me. "We were housed in a dormitory. The college kids were so enthusiastic; they asked a thousand questions and wanted to talk all night. We met Andy Goodman for the first time, and all of us were delighted with him. He was such a fine, intelligent, unassuming young man. He and I had much to talk about because he was a student at my alma mater, Queens College."

Andy Goodman, at twenty, was both like and different from Mickey Schwerner in many ways. His parents, like their parents before them, were humanists in the liberal Jewish tradition. He was not *bar mitzvahed*. He, too, stressed his faith in Man and in social justice in the here and now. Goodman's mother is a psychologist employed by a clinic in Westchester County, New York, and his father is a successful civil engineer and general contractor. Andy was the second of three sons as Mickey was the younger of two.

One difference in the two was in the scope of their commitment to the Movement. Schwerner was a social worker who thought he had found himself in the Movement. Goodman knew that his life had been somewhat sheltered and he believed that his summer in Mississippi would teach him much while at the same time he was determined to make a useful contribution to the Movement. Goodman then, in contrast to Schwerner, the professional reformer, is more representative—if not of the "typical" American—at least of a large group of Americans who recognize an obligation to others, and are willing to work at it but not to devote their entire lives to it, as the professional must.

Goodman's mother explained to me: "Andy knew he had enjoyed most of the good things of life. He was secure in the affections of his brothers, his parents, and his larger family including his grandparents, his uncles, aunts, and cousins. He had been reared in an atmosphere of love, respect, and culture, with books, music, paintings, appreciation of learning, appreciation of individual effort to improve the human personality. He had spent his summers with his cousins and his brothers in our family home in the Adirondacks. He was a happy, well-adjusted, light-hearted young man who knew how and when to be serious. He joined the Movement for two main reasons. He felt it was unfair for him to enjoy so many good things without making some modest effort to help those who are unjustly deprived. And he felt that he had much to learn from the people in Mississippi. He never thought that he had all the answers.

"He had taken part in one demonstration at the World's Fair, and he wanted to work for a summer in Mississippi, after which, had he not been murdered, he would have returned to his studies. He was considering going to Mexico next summer and trying to understand the way of life of the Mexican peasant. Eventually he probably would have wound up as a sociologist or anthropologist, or something in the field of human relations."

Each student going to Mississippi was required to take with him $150 and to have available as much as $500 in bail money.

Goodman's father told me, "I, of course, would gladly have given Andy his money. But he made a point of working for it himself. He wanted his little contribution in Mississippi to be entirely his own."

News of the burning of the church at Longdale reached Mickey Schwerner in Ohio on Wednesday, June 17. It made him anxious to hurry back to Mississippi. He wanted to hold the Freedom School on the site of the burned church, under the scorched trees, with the Negroes sitting on benches which they and workers could build.

Rita Schwerner was urged to remain in Oxford for another week, to help train a second group of summer volunteers. Reluctantly she agreed.

"On Friday night," Rita recalled, "we didn't go to sleep at all. We talked and loaded the station wagon. Four other workers were to travel to Mississippi with Mickey, Jim, and Andy. They left about 3 A.M.—that would be Saturday morning, June 20. They expected to reach Meridian the same day, sometime after dark. Mickey, as usual, was impatient to get going, and all of them were excited and anxious to reach their assigned places and get to work."

"Yes," Rita added, "I did wish that I were going with them. But I stayed . . . and that was the last time I saw Mickey."

SEVEN

On Saturday, June 20, 1964, as Michael Schwerner, James Chaney, Andrew Goodman, and two hundred other student members of the Mississippi Summer Project approached the state from Oxford, Ohio, the United States Senate passed the Civil Rights Bill. So that afternoon and the following Sunday morning the front pages of Mississippi papers looked like this:

CIVIL RIGHTS STEAMROLLER SMASHES ON
Measure Passes Senate 73–27

STRIFE AND CHAOS FORECAST BY PPJ [GOVERNOR JOHNSON]
Barnett: "This action is repulsive to the American people. Turmoil, strife and bloodshed lie ahead."

WALLACE: SAD DAY FOR U.S.
Wallace: "It is ironical that this event occurs as we approach celebration of Independence Day. On that day we won our freedom. On this day we have largely lost it."

On Mississippi radio and television stations there was nothing but angry voices and inflamed faces:

BLOODSHED! STRIFE! TURMOIL! CHAOS!

When leaders predict strife and bloodshed, inevitably, among white-supremacy terrorists, they encourage strife and bloodshed.

Along with this violent reaction to passage of the Civil Rights Bill, here is some of what the people of Mississippi, including the terrorists, were told about the "Summer Invasion":

From Tom Ethridge, a Jackson newspaper columnist:

92

. . . Our guess is that many of the invaders will be surprised to learn that the rank and file of Mississippi Negroes are far more intelligent than is commonly believed in areas from whence cometh these self-important missionaries for "civil rights."

And it will probably come as a shock for them to learn that many Negroes who are registered voters didn't bother to vote in our recent elections which found a number of colored candidates seeking major offices.

Quite a few of the student invaders have preconceived notions about Mississippi . . . hound dogs sleeping in the dust and under shade trees along Capitol Street . . . almost everybody illiterate, ragged, backward, living in hovels, eating sowbelly and cornpone three times daily . . . toting shotguns and plotting secession . . .

In turn, Mississippians have preconceived notions about the invading students—smug, shrill, know-it-all extroverts with a saviour complex . . . problem brats defiant of parental restraint . . . sexually promiscuous, addicted to interracial love-making . . . brainwashed in Communist doctrines with no clear idea of Americanism . . . more hostile to the White South than to Red Russia . . .

It is no preconception but established fact that many of the invading students are coming here from places where racial segregation is the custom, where human life is unsafe on the streets even in broad daylight, and where the local crime rate is among the nation's highest.

Mississippi, in case they don't know it, has had the nation's third lowest rate of major crime . . . according to official FBI figures.

Our parks and streets are generally safe for peaceful, law-abiding people. One can patronize our public transportation facilities without being razored or raped by rat packs like those found in New York, Los Angeles, Chicago and other crime jungles which are furnishing volunteers for this "Project Mississippi" intrusion.

While professing to believe in "equality," these self-appointed reformers evidently regard themselves as mentally and morally superior to Mississippians.

What the students think of us is not very important . . . because the invaders couldn't possibly think less of us than the majority here thinks of them and their sponsors. . . .

From the Dallas *Morning News,* widely reprinted in Mississippi:

. . . The President should now use the force of his office to attack the cause of the trouble in Mississippi. That trouble is the unjustified, uncalled for invasion of that sovereign state by a bunch of Northern students schooled in advance in causing trouble under the guise of bringing "freedom" to Mississippi Negroes.

An editorial in The *Harvard Crimson,* which was given wide circulation in Mississippi, declared that "this summer will witness a massive, daring, probably bloody assault on the racial barriers of Mississippi."

Central to the project, the editorial said, is "the anticipated lawlessness of Mississippi whites. The planners reason that massive non-violence will precipitate a crisis of violence which they consider a prerequisite for further progress."

The invasion of these young busybodies therefore was planned far in advance and, incredibly, has the support of the National Council of Churches.

The students were schooled in invasion at Western College for Women in Oxford, Ohio. The Chicago *Tribune* says they were even taught "how to fall if pushed off lunch counter stools and how to lock themselves into a bundle and make themselves harder to drag away."

One of the lecturers at the school was a gentleman from the Department of Justice who was booed when he told the invaders that the federal government would not promise to protect them.

So there you have it. An "invasion" planned in advance with the announced strategy of creating trouble.

If the people of Mississippi are to be understood, it must not be imagined that they thought they were alone in regarding the invading students as contemptible and Communist-directed. The people of Mississippi believed that their attitude was shared by "Harvard" and by "all decent-thinking Americans." An editorial from the Lowell (Mass.) *Liberator* was widely acclaimed. Here is a portion of it as reprinted:

A thousand college students from the North are reported to be invading Mississippi this summer in order to engage in a Negro voter registration drive. It is unbelievable that a thousand college students would do this of their own volition. Those who know the ways of propaganda, especially of a Communist nature, probably correctly suspect that the idealism of some college youngsters has been taken advantage of by some very hard boiled left wingers and Communists who know exactly what they want to do—stir up trouble in the South.

This newspaper a long time ago pointed out that [a part of the Communist plan in the United States is to stir up racial strife]. The ultimate aim is . . . a black revolution. This invasion of Mississippi this summer is . . . part and parcel of this plan.

These young people who have gone to Mississippi have been attending training schools which can be described as nothing short of inflammatory. . . . The naive inexperience of these youngsters has been preyed on, and they have been stirred up by tales of horror and violence that simply don't exist in Mississippi.

Entirely aside from the arrogance and the holier-than-thou attitude of these college students, who are going to Mississippi with no knowledge of the Negro problem, the really serious aspect of this invasion . . . is [that it] is part of an over-all scheme to destroy the United States by way of a racial revolution.

Most of the people of Mississippi had no idea how unrepresentative of the press outside the South such articles were. Here is another sample, a "Letter from the North" which appeared in many newspapers and was read at many meetings of the Ku Klux Klan and the Citizens Councils:

However Mississippi is maligned, tuck this away in your bright glossary: not one of my circle of . . . acquaintances —not one—but has a feeling of sympathy . . . for Mississippians; nor does any of these sympathizers regard the imbecilic, fatuous fatheads invading Mississippi from the North as anything but troublemakers—unsavory whifflebirds possessed of all the high . . . intellectual attributes of . . . primeval octopods dredged up from some old, abandoned cesspool and foisted upon innocent natives.

So those who were plotting to combat the Invasion by murdering Mickey Schwerner thought of themselves as patriots. Klan meetings are normally opened with a prayer. Among the members of most Klan groups are many fundamentalist preachers, for a peculiar religious fervor is typical of the organization. The conspirators had been told that the Lord was on their side, that the murder of Schwerner would please God.

. . .

Sunday, June 21, 1964, was the longest day in the year. In Mississippi it was sunny and hot. The blue Ford station wagon had reached Meridian about 8:30 P.M. on Saturday, and Mickey Schwerner, Andy Goodman, and several others had slept in the dilapidated upstairs apartment at 1308 34th Avenue. Goodman had slept in a sleeping bag he had brought.

Sue Brown, the young Negro woman with whom I talked in New Jersey in October, told me:

"With Rita having remained in Ohio for another week, I was in charge of the Community Center. We knew that Mickey and Jim had returned on Saturday night with several new people, so we all began to gather at the Center around eight-thirty on Sunday morning. Mickey and Andy Goodman ate breakfast at the café across the street. Everybody was excited. We were meeting the new people who were going to spend the summer helping us, and a lot of questions were being asked. Mickey and Andy reached the Center first, then Jim Chaney came in. He had slept at his mother's home, where he lived. Mickey was full of ideas and enthusiasms, but the main thing on his mind was Longdale. He knew several of the Longdale people had been beaten up, and he wanted to visit them. He wanted the Longdale people to meet Andy, and he wanted to make plans to hold the Freedom School up there on the grounds of the burned church."

I asked: "But didn't Mickey indicate that he regarded the trip to Longdale as dangerous? Much more dangerous than anything he had done yet? The church's ashes were only five days old. The woman's broken collarbone had not had time to mend. It was the first day after passage of the Civil Rights Bill, the day when redneck tempers would be hottest. It was the first day of the 'Summer Invasion.' And Longdale was the first place where Mickey's operations had met with violence. Didn't he indicate in some manner that he understood all this?"

"Yes, I think he was more serious than I had ever seen him before," Miss Brown said. "He knew that the telephone calls threatening him with death had become more numerous. And he read the newspapers."

"Then why did he go? Why didn't he wait two or three days and study the reaction to the Summer Project and the Civil Rights Bill? Why didn't he wait and let one of the Negroes from Longdale drive to Meridian and describe the situation to him? He had a lot of work to do in Meridian, organizing his new people. Why did he insist on putting his head in the lion's mouth on the first day? Didn't you urge him to wait? Didn't Chaney urge him to wait?"

Sue Brown reflected, shook her head. "Ours wasn't a waiting operation," she said. "Our word was NOW. Freedom NOW. Mickey was serious. He was concerned. He knew that going to Longdale was dangerous. But those people up there had taken risks and suffered, and he thought he ought to go. He *wanted* to go. He took some precautions. Three or four other people asked to go with him, but he narrowed them down to Jim and Andy. About nine-thirty or close to ten he sat down with me and went over the travel plan. He said he had a few things to do in Meridian, like getting his hair cut and the car serviced, but that he expected to be in Longdale by noon, he'd spend about three hours up there, and he'd be back at the Center at four P.M."

"Maybe I had a premonition," Sue Brown continued. "I remember asking him: 'If you're not back at four, what time do I start calling?' He answered: 'At four-thirty. But we'll be back by four.'"

While a young Negro student barber cut Mickey's hair, Jim Chaney and Andy Goodman had the station wagon serviced at a Negro-owned filling station. I questioned Rita Schwerner about the condition of the station wagon.

"It was kept in excellent condition," she said. "We of course understood that a tire or engine failure at the wrong time and place could be fatal. We had bought two new tires in April: I later found the purchase slip. It was a dark blue, four-door Ford wagon, 1963 model, with about forty thousand miles on it. The license number was H 25 503."

As always, the gasoline tank was filled full in Meridian. Schwerner and Chaney did not know of a friendly service station in Neshoba County, and they knew that a stop in a strange service station could mean trouble. They understood that the three would be conspicuous travelers on a Sunday in Mississippi. First, because of dress: all three were hatless and wore the COFO "uniform" of T-shirt, blue jeans, and sneakers. Second, because Schwerner wore a beard. And third, because they were two young white men traveling with a young Negro man, all sitting on the front seat, with the Negro driving.

What about the terrorists? What had they been doing since their frustration and near-shootout at the Longdale church?

On the morning after they burned the church, the Meridian group learned that Schwerner was not in the city, and they had been watching for him. On Saturday night, minutes after the station wagon reached 1308 34th Avenue, they knew he was back. On Sunday morning they saw him in the café, and they saw the station wagon being serviced. Did they guess he was going to Longdale on Sunday afternoon? Were they so informed?

The answer seems to be: probably not. Sometime between 1 and 3 P.M. Deputy Sheriff Cecil Price, who was at Philadelphia, knew that Schwerner and two companions were at Longdale. Apparently this tip reached Price almost exactly at

3 P.M. because that is when he began acting on it. If a car from Meridian had followed the station wagon, the terrorists would have tipped Price off much earlier—within a few minutes after the station wagon reached Longdale. According to Longdale Negroes, the station wagon reached Longdale a little before 1 P.M.

There is another point. Before he arrested the three, Price thought that the Negro with Schwerner was George Raymond, prominent in the Movement at Canton. Price associated Raymond with the station wagon. After the wagon had been used at Canton in February, a leaflet carrying a picture of Raymond had also carried the picture of the station wagon. Raymond was much more prominent than Chaney, and therefore more hated. When Price trailed the station wagon and stopped it, he thought he was catching Schwerner and Raymond and "another Jew-boy." Not until he confronted Chaney did Price learn that the Negro with Schwerner was not George Raymond.

This could mean that Price's tipster mistook Chaney for Raymond and so misinformed Price. But would a Meridian tipster have made such a mistake? He might have. But since Chaney lived in Meridian and had become such a close associate of Schwerner, this seems unlikely.

There is another possibility: that Price's tipster didn't tell Price who the Negro was, and Price simply guessed that the Negro was Raymond.

My own opinion is that no Meridian group learned or guessed on Sunday morning that Schwerner was going to Neshoba County. I believe the tip to Price came from someone in the Longdale area.

Here, the question kept recurring to me: By COFO's own standards, was Schwerner's decision to visit Neshoba County that Sunday a reckless decision? In the particular time and manner in which he risked three lives was Mickey Schwerner, in some degree, blameworthy? He was not, like Goodman, a "college kid." He was an experienced social worker with five months in Mississippi. Was there something unique about Mickey Schwerner which caused him alone to make the decision which resulted in the only deaths suffered by COFO workers in Mississippi?

I put the question to Geoffrey Wiener, the executive director of Hamilton-Madison House, who had hired Mickey.

"Yes," Mr. Wiener said, "I think Mickey's impulse to visit Longdale on June twenty-first might have been predicted by those of us who knew and admired him. He felt this tremendous devotion to minority groups—to anybody in trouble. He was uncompromising. But all of us sensed a certain immaturity about him. There was defiance in his personality . . . a drive to get into the middle of things . . . and on his return to Mississippi from Oxford, Ohio, I guess I would have predicted that Mickey would be the one who immediately, and perhaps without proper preparation, tackled his most dangerous problem. At Hamilton-Madison House he was impatient unless he was working with the roughest youngsters. He seemed to need to prove his manhood to himself. Speaking analytically, not critically, I think it is fair to say that Mickey, more than most men in his profession, may have had a yearning for martyrdom."

Rita Schwerner did not agree with Mr. Wiener. "By June 1964 I don't think there was anything immature about Mickey," she said. "I was not with him when he made the decision to go to Longdale, but I understand why he made it. In Oxford he had been told only that the church in Longdale had been burned. He had not been told that people had been beaten. Only after he reached Meridian did he learn of the beatings. Once he learned that people in Longdale had suffered physical harm for trying to cooperate with him, for him not to have gone up there would have been a breach of faith. He wanted to learn the extent of their injuries, and to help them. In his position he had to go."

Though no one is certain, Schwerner, Chaney, and Goodman seem to have traveled from Meridian to Longdale by the nearest route. They went up Highway 19, crossed the Neshoba county line, then turned due north on a dirt road, Highway 491. This road intersects east–west Highway 16 about two miles east of Longdale. So to reach Longdale they would have turned west on 16.

At Longdale they inspected the site of the burned church, then visited at some length at four Negro houses. The Negroes told them about the unmasked white men, about the beatings and the burning, and Schwerner was told that the white men had been looking for him. He was warned, gravely warned, and this warning may be the answer to a question which has puzzled all who have studied this case.

At 3:51 P.M. why was the station wagon on Highway 16 headed *west* for Philadelphia? Schwerner had told Sue Brown he'd be at the Community Center at Meridian at 4 P.M. He was a man who followed travel plans rigidly. The shortest route back to Meridian was the way they had come. Going toward Philadelphia from Longdale was going *away* from Meridian! Why did Schwerner, running behind schedule, decide to return to Meridian by way of Philadelphia?

There is a quick, easy answer. It was a bright, hot Sunday afternoon. Goodman had never been in Mississippi. He had come to work in Neshoba County. Highway 16 is a broad, heavily traveled highway. So is 19. Maybe the sight of Sunday traffic caused Schwerner and Chaney to relax their fears. Maybe at the cost of being a few minutes late in Meridian,

NESHOBA COUNTY

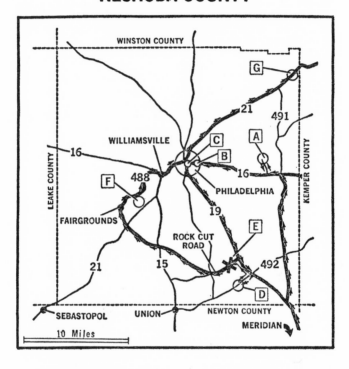

A. Visited Longdale Church	E. Murder Scene
B. Victims Arrested	F. Bodies Buried Here
C. Released From Jail	G. Station Wagon Taken
D. Victims' Car Overtaken	Here & Burned

they decided to go via Philadelphia and show Goodman more of the county he would be working in. Maybe it's that simple.

Here is the more likely answer. When Schwerner received the warning in Longdale, he and Chaney recognized the possibility that they had been followed from Meridian. Or noticed and reported as they came up 491. If they returned on 491, they could be blocked by two pickup trucks and grabbed: it's a comparatively narrow "back" road. But on neither 16 nor 19, on a Sunday afternoon, could they be blocked—except by the law. So they chose to risk being blocked by the law on a main highway rather than risk being blocked by terrorists on a back road.

About 3:15 P.M. Highway Patrolmen Poe and Wiggs were sitting under a shade tree alongside Highway 16 about a mile east of the Philadelphia city limit. The temperature had hit 101; so Poe and Wiggs had parked their car, left their belts and pistols on the back seat, and got out to cool in the shade. Their white patrol car was clearly visible from the highway. From where they were sitting they could hear the radio which connected them with all other police cars within forty miles and with the patrol substation at Meridian.

Price drove past them, headed east, in his 1957 Chevrolet. Poe and Wiggs knew he saw their car, and when he didn't stop they cocked their ears toward their radio, expecting some word from him. He said nothing to them, and in a few minutes they saw the station wagon, driving west, with Price tailing but not *chasing* it. They noted that the station wagon was not speeding.

A few minutes thereafter Poe and Wiggs heard Price on the radio asking them to join him in front of the First Methodist Church to "help transport three subjects to jail." Price had trailed the station wagon past the city limit, then had sounded his siren and stopped both the station wagon and his car in a wide parking area at the church. Price got out of his car, and in response to his order the three got out of the station wagon. He told them they were under arrest but apparently did not tell them what for. Price, as well as the three, noticed that a rear tire on the station wagon was almost flat. Price told them to change tires; and when Poe and Wiggs arrived in the state car, Chaney, Schwerner, and Goodman were changing tires as Price stood by.

In the hearing of the two state patrolmen Goodman asked Price what they were under arrest for. Price replied, "Investigation."

Price later declared that he arrested Chaney for "speeding" and arrested Schwerner and Goodman for "suspicion of arson," meaning that he suspected them of burning the Long-dale church. Price knew that Schwerner and Goodman didn't burn the church; and, under the circumstances, of all the ve-hicles in Mississippi that Sunday afternoon, the station wagon was the least likely to have been speeding.

When the spare tire had been put on the station wagon, Price told Schwerner and Goodman to get in the back seat of the state patrol car. Poe then got under the wheel of the state car where he noticed that he was not wearing his gun. He had left it on the back seat. He turned to get it and found Schwerner in the act of handing it to him.

"When those boys got in the back seat," Poe said, "Schwerner either had to sit on that .357 Magnum with its holster and belt or pick it up. He had picked it up and was handing it to me, just to do me a favor. I guess that's the first time a prisoner ever handed me my own gun."

Officer Wiggs got in the station wagon with Chaney, and Wiggs did the driving. Price, alone in his car, which was an old 1957 blue Chevrolet trimmed in white, led the way, and the three-car caravan moved along eleven city blocks to the new, single-story Neshoba county jail.

There was nothing secret about the arrest. It occurred in broad daylight, on Sunday afternoon. Three cars stood in front of the Methodist Church for at least twenty minutes. Many motorists passed, slowed down, looked; and some of them turned around and passed again, to get closer looks. There were motorists who recognized the three young men as "civil rights workers"—from Schwerner's beard, from the blue jeans and the sneakers, from the presence of the Negro. The procession to the jail attracted attention: it looked as if dangerous criminals, Most Wanted Men, had been appre-hended. The station wagon was not parked in front of the Neshoba county jail, but in front of the city hall, a half-block away.

When they were booked into the county jail, the three met Mr. and Mrs. H. V. M. Herring, a middle-aged couple who are the jailers. Mrs. Herring is a formidable character. She has many relatives and friends in Neshoba County, some of whom are Ku Klux. She can call a man a "gawddam son-ofabitch" as fiercely as any lady I ever met.

Mrs. Herring booked Schwerner and Goodman as "Negroes" along with Chaney, but Schwerner and Goodman were lodged together in a front cell with another white pris-oner. Chaney was lodged in a back cell with another Negro prisoner.

All three officers, Price, Poe, and Wiggs, left the jail as

soon as the three were locked in. In their two cars they drove around the block which separated the jail from the court-house. Poe and Wiggs parked the state car on the north side of the courthouse. The time was about 4:20 P.M.

Poe and Wiggs saw their superior, Inspector King, of the highway patrol, come out of a drugstore. They motioned for

INSIDE OF THE JAIL

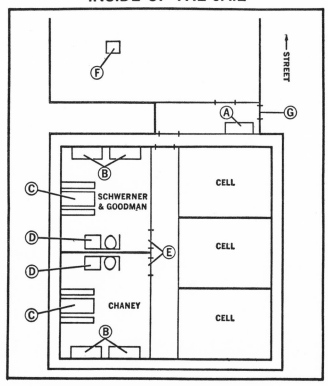

A. **Desk Where Booked**   D. **Shower-Toilet**
B. **Bunks,**   E. **Cell Doors**
   Upper-Lower   F. **Herring's Phone**
C. **Metal Table**   G. **Entrance to Jail**

him to come to their car, and he joined them. They told him about Price arresting the three COFO workers.

While the patrol officers sat in the patrol car talking, Price walked up and got into the back seat of the patrol car. King asked him what he intended doing with the COFO workers. Price replied that he planned to hold them seventy-two hours —that he understood he could legally hold them that long for investigation.

So at 4:30 P.M., the time Sue Brown was to begin calling if the three had not returned to the Community Center, the three were locked in the Neshoba county jail. Many persons knew this, including an inspector. In fact it is probable that the highway patrolmen thought the three boys were in jail all night long. But highway patrolmen have radios, and they usually report arrests in which they have a part. Did they report this perilous situation to any of their superiors?

EIGHT

For most normal human beings, including those in Mississippi, much of what follows will be incomprehensible. Again it's like Auschwitz. Many people, including Germans, can't yet comprehend Auschwitz. They know it happened, but they can't believe it. Mercifully perhaps, the normal mind shrinks from comprehending murder planned on behalf of a state.

On Sunday evening, June 21, 1964, many of the people of Mississippi went to church. They prayed, and sang the old songs of faith and hope, and tried to feel some measure of forgiveness toward the United States: toward Earl Warren, and Lyndon Johnson, even Martin Luther King. These church people tried not to hate the National Council of Churches for sending the "Dirty T-Shirts" to try to help Mississippi's Negroes. In their hearts these Mississippi church people tried to accept the Civil Rights Act as the law of the land.

Other good people in Mississippi visited their parents because it was Father's Day. Others went bowling, or to drive-in movies, and kissed and made love because they were young and it was hot summertime and there was an almost-full moon which didn't set until 2:36 A.M. Others, like Justice of the Peace Leonard Warren, of Philadelphia, watched television—Ed Sullivan and *Bonanza* and *What's My Line?*—and went to bed "as soon as the good programs were over." Still others, like Sheriff Rainey, visited relatives in hospitals. The sheriff's wife had been in a Meridian hospital for several days. He was concerned about her, and his two young sons without their mother. He had had a cot placed in her room, and one or two nights he had slept in the hospital room with her, then sped back to his job in Philadelphia, thirty-six miles away.

But perhaps as many as forty citizens of Mississippi spent Sunday evening committing a criminal act against the United States of America.

105

These citizens, with the help of "the law," committed a planned murder for the purpose of dramatizing Mississippi's defiance of the laws of the United States!

"When this night's over," a citizen declared, "they'll know how Mississippi stands. They'll know we're not gonna take it! Not now or ever! They're not gonna cram niggers into our schools or restaurants, and no more niggers are gonna vote in Mississippi. Martin Luther King may run the rest of the country, but he ain't gonna run Mississippi. And every Communist-atheist-nigger-loving-bearded-Jew-sonofabitch who comes down here looking for trouble is gonna find it!"

The men who planned and committed this murder thought they were acting, not *against* the state of Mississippi, but *for* Mississippi *against* the United States.

When any group of citizens acts illegally within a state, if the state makes no effort to punish them, the group claims to have acted on behalf of the state. This was true in the Weimar Republic. A group of German citizens (Nazis) acted illegally by assaulting and murdering their opponents. The state, or local agents of the state, failed to act against these terrorists, thereby giving effective approval of the illegal actions and encouraging other such actions. As could have been predicted, the Nazis took over the state itself.

The terrorists seem unlikely to take over Mississippi; but so long as Mississippi remains powerless to punish them, the terrorists will continue to believe they are acting for the state.

The murderers of Michael Schwerner, Andrew Goodman, and James Chaney acted like the Nazis in the Weimar Republic. While their less active neighbors sang hymns, watched television, made love, or slept, the terrorists struck a blow for "states' rights" against the "federal tyranny"; and since so many of the neighbors approve the action, the state lacks the power to punish, disclaim, or even denounce it. The murderers therefore consider themselves, and are widely regarded as, patriots.

This murder was no ordinary outrage committed by one human being against another and therefore against a *state*. It was part of the continuing war between Mississippi terrorists and the United States of America. Once this is understood comprehension of what happened may become easier.

• • •

Sheriff's Deputy Cecil Price believed he was protecting the state of Mississippi, and acting in its best interest, when he arrested Michael Schwerner and when he delivered him to his murderers. So by 5 P.M. the conspirators were on the move:

first in Neshoba County, then in Lauderdale County, conferring, planning, preparing to "activate Plan Four" and "exterminate the Jew-boy with the beard."

The arrest of Goodman and Chaney with Schwerner had not been anticipated. So a conference was held in Meridian to decide what to do with "the coon and the other Jew." The fate of Schwerner had been sealed when he entered the Neshoba county jail: he'd come out only to be killed. But the fate of Chaney and Goodman was not decided until around 7 P.M., in Meridian.

There was an argument Franz Kafka would have appreciated. Some of the conspirators did *not* want to murder Chaney. They didn't think a "goddam Mississippi coon is worth all this trouble we're going to."

"What the hell!" one of them argued. "We can shoot that black sonofabitch down on the street here in Meridian any night. Why should we go to all this trouble to kill a Mississippi coon?"

The point they were debating is this: To kill Schwerner and hide his body, this group of "patriots" were going to an almost disgraceful amount of "trouble." They were going to stay up most of the night, stage an elaborate cat-and-mouse chase, and wait around for a bulldozer to bury a body in a dam. Why the hell should they dignify a mere "Mississippi coon" with that much trouble?

Of all the discriminations he suffered in life, none was as paradoxical as the one James Chaney almost suffered in death. The patriots almost rejected him as "not worth killing . . . not worth all this trouble." They allowed him to die with Schwerner only because they couldn't figure how to turn him loose without his knowing too much.

Goodman's case was similar, but with a difference. The conspirators had never heard of Goodman: they didn't know his name. Most of them didn't know Schwerner's name either, but for months they had been hating him as "the Jew-boy with the beard." Goodman was a newcomer: the Meridian terrorists had not had time to learn to hate him personally. They were told from Philadelphia that "the other Jew don't even wear a beard." They were even told "The other Jew don't look much like a Jew." The "patriots" had no moral objections to including "another atheist, Communist, nigger-loving Jew" among their victims, but Goodman would have escaped if they could have "figured how to turn him loose without him knowing too much."

What may have cost Chaney and Goodman their lives was the fact that Chaney was driving the station wagon when the three were arrested. If Schwerner had been driving, he could have been charged with speeding and the other two could have been held on "suspicion" or for "investigation." (Only the driver of a vehicle can be charged with speeding, not passengers.) Then when the murderers were assembled and ready down on Highway 19, Schwerner alone could have been "released after payment of a fine," and he, alone in the station wagon, could have been directed down Highway 19 to his death. The other two could have been held until morning, then released, without their knowing much.

Did Schwerner, Chaney, or Goodman worry while they were in jail? Did they anticipate what was to happen to them?

Highway Patrolmen Wiggs and Poe, who helped transport them to jail, said they didn't appear worried at that time. "They couldn't have acted nicer," the patrolmen said. "They were nice boys."

The Negro prisoner who shared a cell with Chaney for about five hours said that Chaney went to sleep about four-thirty, woke up for supper at six, then went back to sleep. The white prisoner who shared the cell with Schwerner and Goodman said they "whispered together a good deal" but didn't seem scared to him.

Since the three are dead, this is one of several questions which can never be answered positively. But my guess is that they didn't worry much until they were told they were to be "freed," which may have been as late as 10:15 P.M. Even during battles I have noted that few young men can anticipate their own deaths.

True, Schwerner and Chaney had been warned at Longdale. They knew enough to be afraid of Price. But they must have found the presence of the highway patrolmen reassuring. When they were denied the opportunity to use a telephone, the three may have felt fearful. But Schwerner knew that by 4:30 P.M. Sue Brown had telephoned the COFO office in Jackson and with each passing hour he knew that telephones were ringing all over Mississippi, even in Washington. A Justice Department attorney was staying at Holiday Inn in Meridian; and I imagine Schwerner expected him to walk into the Neshoba county jail by 9 P.M.

What Schwerner could not know was that no one who was friendly to him knew he was in Neshoba county jail. By 5:30 P.M. COFO workers had called the jail and the sheriff's office, and they had been told that the three had not been seen. Moreover, the highway patrol offices at both Meridian and Jackson denied any knowledge of the three. Had Schwerner known that all the telephoning was proving ineffective, he would have been more worried. Not only were the three being held incommunicado, but their arrest was also being denied. The COFO workers were being given false information by Neshoba County; and the COFO workers could not persuade either the highway patrol or the FBI or the Justice Department to communicate with Neshoba County.

One telephone call before 10 P.M. to the Neshoba County jail or sheriff's office from either a state or federal official probably could have halted proceedings. But it was a long, hot Sunday evening, and where was there any evidence of crime?

Any highway patrol car moving along Highway 19 between Meridian and Philadelphia early Sunday evening must have noted unusual activity. Darkness came late, but by eight-thirty the men had begun to gather. At a point about ten miles south of Philadelphia there is a "wide place in the road" on Highway 19. There is a filling station, several houses, and a dirt road turns off to the right, going west. This road is called Rock Cut Road because a portion of it near Highway 19 was cut through a hill, and there are high rock banks on both sides. This is where the "patriots" were gathering; and they were unusually excited because the three "rats" were soon to be let out of the trap up at Philadelphia. They were then to be "run down again" and murdered. It was like waiting along a race course for the racers to pass. Moreover, this group included some of the same playful boys with their guns who had almost "shot it out" with one another at Longdale. Tension was high. I was told that the murderers got so excited while they waited that they "were running around down there like wild men."

There was a loud argument over who would have the honor of "pulling the trigger" on the "two Jews and the coon." Blows or shots were avoided only by deciding to "share the honor" by "passing the gun around."

The situation threatened to get out of hand, so about nine forty-five, when action became imminent, several carloads of men were ordered to go home. This had the effect of removing most of the older men from the scene and leaving a group of young toughs, averaging about Schwerner's own age, to do "the killing and the burying." This is standard operating procedure for terrorists as well as for most armies. When the chips go down and blood must flow, leave the young ones to do it.

They enjoy it more.

My most serious error was in my account of this "gathering" of conspirators and murderers south of Philadelphia, along Highway 19 and on Rock Cut Road. I did not exaggerate the number of men who knew that Schwerner was to be killed. But because my informants exaggerated, I did exaggerate the number of men who got in cars, and drove somewhere and assembled.

James Jordan, a Klansman who became an FBI informer, testified at the trial that on the afternoon of June 21, 1964, he went to the Long Horn Cafe, which was operated in Meridian by one of the defendants, Frank Herndon. At the cafe Jordan said he found Rev. Edgar Ray Killen, James Harris, Jerry Sharpe and "another young man." Jordan said Killen said he had a job to do and he needed some help, that they had two or three civil rights workers locked up there (in Neshoba County) and they needed their rear-ends tore up.

Jordan said they made a number of telephone calls from the cafe (seeking to recruit Klansmen for the job), then went to B. L. Akin's Mobile Homes to make more calls "because they didn't want a crowd gathering at the Longhorn."

"I told Killen I'd go and try to find a couple of men that I knew who didn't have telephones," Jordan testified. He said he went to Alton Wayne Roberts and told him they needed help and asked if he'd go. He said he returned to Akin's place and found Akin, Harris, Roberts, Travis Barnette, Horace Doyle Barnette, James Snowden, Killen, Sharpe and Jimmy Arledge. Jordan said: "At that time Killen said the civil rights workers were locked up and they were to be turned loose and we were to pick them up and tear their butts up."

Jordan said Killen, Sharpe and Roberts then left in one car, while he, Snowden, Arledge, and Horace Doyle Barnette left in another car. He said they went to the side of the courthouse in Philadelphia and saw Hop Barnette (the present sheriff) standing beside his pickup truck. He quoted Barnette as telling them to wait there, that someone would come and tell them what to do.

Jordan said Killen then came by and showed them a place to wait "behind an old warehouse." Jordan said that as they waited a police car stopped and "the driver told us they [the civil rights workers] were going toward Meridian on 19." Jordan said they followed a red car in front and the car pulled up alongside a "patrol car."

Jordan said that Billy Wayne Posey was in the other car and told them it was "all right, we weren't going to have to stop them, the deputy was going to stop them."

Jordan said they followed at high speed, and then saw the

lights ahead and that "the deputy had the three people stopped."

I now come to the area of this story which is most difficult to explain and where what appears to have been the conduct of the victims becomes hard to understand. Much of the difficulty, no doubt, derives from the fact that information is missing, information which may never be obtained.

It is 10 P.M. The killers are assembled ten miles south of Philadelphia, waiting for the victims to be delivered. It is time to let them out of the jail, for the telephone call to be made to the killers alerting them that the Ford station wagon will soon reach the point where it is to be run down again.

The station wagon is standing in partial darkness a few feet down a hill from the front of the Philadelphia city hall and half a block from the front of the Neshoba county jail. The street in front of the jail, Myrtle Street, is well lighted; there is also a bright moon; and half a block from the jail is the Benwalt Hotel, which is open, and in its lobby are two public telephones. The hotel is clearly visible, easily noticed, from the front of the jail.

First, here is the Rainey-Price explanation of what happened. It has been published repeatedly throughout the world, and it was given to me in detail by Sheriff Rainey:

RAINEY: Well, I wasn't here. I was in Meridian at the hospital with my wife. But I believe what my deputy says. He had arrested the nigger for speeding. He was holding the other two for investigation. Normally, he would have carried the nigger before a justice of the peace where he would have paid the fine and been turned loose. But this was Sunday afternoon. So sometime during that evening Price telephoned Justice of the Peace Leonard Warren, and Warren told him to collect twenty dollars from the nigger and let him go. And that's what he did. Price turned all three of them out, let them get in their car, and start off toward Meridian. A city officer, Richard Willis, was with Price; and Willis and Price followed the station wagon down to the city limits on Highway 19. The last that Willis and Price saw of those three was their taillights disappearing down 19 toward Meridian.

Then here is some of the language of a federal grand jury indictment returned against Price, Rainey, and sixteen others: *

* The press reported that the federal government had two confessions. However, seventeen of the eighteen defendants pleaded not guilty.

JAILHOUSE AREA IN PHILADELPHIA

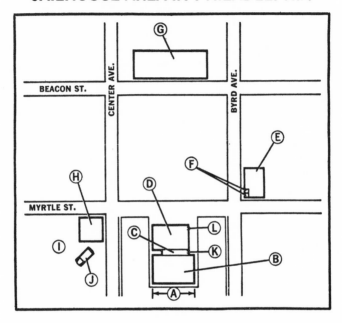

A. Neshoba County Jail

B. Cells

C. Lobby

D. Jailer's Quarters

E. Benwalt Hotel

F. Phone Booths

G. Courthouse

H. City Hall & Police Dept.

I. Parking Area

J. Station Wagon Parked Here

K. Entrance to Jail

L. Entrance to Jailer's Quarters

It was part of the plan and purpose of the conspiracy that Cecil Ray Price, while having Michael Henry Schwerner, James Earl Chaney and Andrew Goodman in custody in the Neshoba County Jail located in Philadelphia, Mississippi, would release them from custody at such time that he, Cecil Ray Price, Jimmy Arledge, Horace Doyle Barnette, Travis Maryn Barnette, Alton Wayne Roberts, Jimmy Snowden, James E. Jordan, Billy Wayne Posey and Jerry McGrew Sharpe could and would intercept Michael Henry Schwerner, James Earl Chaney and Andrew Goodman upon their leaving the area of the jail, and threaten, assault, shoot and kill them....

Pursuant to the conspiracy, and in furtherance of the objects thereof, the following defendants committed the following overt acts within the Southern District of Mississippi:

On June 21, 1964, Cecil Ray Price detained Michael Henry Schwerner, James Earl Chaney and Andrew Goodman in the Neshoba County Jail located in Philadelphia, Mississippi, after sundown on that day until approximately 10:30 P.M.

On June 21, 1964, Billy Wayne Posey drove an automobile south on Highway 19 from Philadelphia, Mississippi.

On June 21, 1964, Cecil Ray Price drove an automobile south on Highway 19 from Philadelphia, Mississippi.

On June 21, 1964, Cecil Ray Price removed Michael Henry Schwerner, James Earl Chaney and Andrew Goodman from an automobile stopped on Highway 492 between Highway 19 and Union, Mississippi, and placed them in an official automobile of the Neshoba County Sheriff's office.

On June 21, 1964, Cecil Ray Price transported Michael Henry Schwerner, James Earl Chaney and Andrew Goodman from a place on State Highway 492 between Highway 19 and Union, Mississippi, to a place on an unpaved road intersecting Highway 19 and south of Philadelphia, Mississippi [Rock Cut Road].

On June 21, 1964, Billy Wayne Posey drove an automobile bearing the bodies of Michael Henry Schwerner, James Earl Chaney and Andrew Goodman from a place on an unpaved road intersecting Highway 19 south of Philadelphia, Mississippi, to the vicinity of the construction site of an earthen dam, located near Highway 21, approximately 5 miles southwest of Philadelphia, Mississippi.

(This indictment was dismissed in 1966. Subsequently a second indictment was returned charging nineteen men with "conspiring to violate the civil rights" of the three murder victims. Murder, unless committed on federal property, is not a federal crime.)

From the day I began work on this story I have doubted that Schwerner, Chaney and Goodman were ever, for one moment, "free" after they were arrested. I find it difficult to believe that at ten, ten-fifteen, or ten-thirty, on being told they were free, Michael Schwerner would *willingly* have led the other two from the jail, walked to the parked station wagon, entered it and driven off toward Meridian.

Why would he have acted in such a manner? He had been warned at Longdale. He had watched darkness fall. He must have assumed they were relatively safe in jail. He assumed that telephoning was being done, that help was on its way. Wouldn't Schwerner have refused to leave the jail? The three were trained in "lie-in" tactics: how to protect themselves from blows, how to go limp and make themselves difficult to carry away. If they had refused to leave the jail, what could the murderers have done?

Is it possible that when they were not mistreated in jail Schwerner came to believe that they would be allowed to leave Neshoba County unharmed? Then what about the telephone? Once Schwerner was told he was free, he certainly must have asked to use the telephone. This is what he himself had emphasized to all the students at Oxford, Ohio. And if, while being assured he was free, he was denied permission to use the jail telephone, would not he *then* have suspected what was afoot?

If Schwerner, at ten-thirty, had walked free from the jail into Myrtle Street, after having been denied the privilege of using the jail telephone, would not his first steps have been toward the Benwalt Hotel and a public telephone? Why would he have turned toward that station wagon which was so obviously a potential trap?

Because of such questions, from the beginning I insisted that the three must have been marched from the jail in handcuffs, perhaps placed in the station wagon, and that one of the murderers then drove the station wagon to the murder scene. But other men said this:

"No, Price didn't dare march them out of jail. It was still too early on Sunday evening. There was too much light. Too many people knew they were there. The conspirators didn't dare seize them when they entered the station wagon. No, Price and the gang had to take the calculated risk of turning them loose and running them down again."

"But that calculated risk," I insisted, "was too big a risk for the planners to take. The three could have escaped. Remember the trip Ed Pitt took to Neshoba County with Chaney? How Chaney drove like the wind and would stop for *nothing*? How Chaney felt sorry for anything that got in front of the car? If Chaney had ever been given control of that station wagon again and allowed to head down Highway 19, nothing short of a bullet would ever have stopped him.

The conspirators didn't use a roadblock: the road was too wide and heavily traveled. Are you saying that Price, in that 1957 Chevrolet, could have given Chaney a start in that 1963 Ford, then run him down? Chaney would never have stopped that station wagon until it was wrecked or he had been shot. Price would have assumed this and would never have risked it."

"There are points you are forgetting," I was told. "Chaney without Schwerner, drove like a young Mississippi Negro. He exceeded speed limits. But with Schwerner in the car, Chaney had to consider Schwerner's feelings. Schwerner was the level-headed advocate of nonviolence. He wouldn't even let young Negroes wear tiny chains around their necks. He thought somebody might consider such a chain a weapon (if wrapped around knuckles). So when Schwerner was with him Chaney didn't exceed speed limits. Price probably told the three that when they left the jail, for their own safety, they must walk directly to the station wagon. Price probably walked with them. I think Price told them that, again for their own safety, he would 'escort' the station wagon to the county line. Maybe when they reached the station wagon it was Schwerner, not Chaney, who took the wheel and did the driving. Chaney didn't drive all the time. When he was with Schwerner, they took turns driving. Whichever one was driving, I believe the station wagon was driven within the speed limit all the way from the jail to where it was stopped. And I believe the station wagon stopped the moment an official car signaled it to stop."

Rita Schwerner agreed with much of this theory. "It's true," she said, "that Mickey made a point of never exceeding speed limits in Mississippi. He was a good driver. He liked to drive. In New York and out West he had been arrested several times for speeding. But when we reached Mississippi he knew that exceeding speed limits was a luxury he couldn't afford. Despite his being watched more carefully than other drivers, in all our five months in Mississippi, he never received any sort of traffic ticket. When he was with Jim Chaney, they took turns driving. Mickey never thought of himself as Jim's boss. Maybe Mickey did drive away from the jail. If Chaney drove, I think he and Mickey would have discussed what to do, and Chaney might or might not have followed Mickey's wishes.

"As to why they left the jail," Rita said, "I think that, to the extent that they had a choice, Mickey would have done whatever he thought offered them the best hope of getting out of Neshoba County without being hurt. I think he would have decided that following the orders of officials of the state of Mississippi would be their best hope. I'm sure Mickey felt afraid in the Neshoba county jail. Particularly when he was refused the right to telephone. But he believed that help was on the way; and if he was told by Price to leave the jail and drive away in the station wagon, I think he would have done just that. How could he have imagined what was afoot? Ninety-nine per cent of the people of Neshoba County claim that they could not have imagined it."

In any case the three left the Neshoba county jail; the station wagon left where it had been parked, and it was not stopped again until it reached a point west of Highway 19 on Highway 492. And this raises all my old questions again. After leaving Philadelphia on Highway 19, the station wagon passed the waiting conspirators at Rock Cut Road and traveled four miles farther south. Then it made a sharp right turn off of Highway 19 and onto 492. Why would it have turned had it not been trying to elude pursuit? There is a dispute as to whether the station wagon made this turn at high speed or at moderate speed. FBI agents were observed testing the turn, one car pursuing another, trying to determine the maximum speed at which the turn could be made.

Does this mean that when the "official car" mentioned in the indictment began signaling for the station wagon to stop —when the police car began sounding its siren and flashing its red light—Chaney, if he was driving, instinctively accelerated and tried to outrun the pursuers?

"It has to mean that," Sue Brown said. "If James Chaney was driving . . . if he knew that they had not been allowed to telephone at the jail . . . if he had been followed all the way from Philadelphia by the police car . . . if he had been driving under the speed limit . . . and if the police car then makes a run at him, signaling him to stop . . . James Chaney just naturally *has* to run! He *knows* what they are stopping him for! He doesn't have a doubt in the world! So he can't do anything but run."

If that is true, why didn't Chaney stay on 19 and try to make the Lauderdale County line? From the intersection of 19 and 492, the county line is six miles away on 19 and eight miles away on 492.

"I know why Chaney would turn," Sue Brown said. "He knew some dirt roads which turn off of 492. He knew these roads well. He'd figure that he could turn into one of these dirt roads and escape."

Then why didn't the station wagon turn into a dirt road?

Why did it stop, on the pavement, less than two miles after it had turned onto 492?

A partial answer might be this: maybe the lead car in pursuit, at that point, was another car and much faster than the Price's 1957 Chevrolet?

Even so, why did the station wagon stop? Why didn't it force the pursuers to employ gunfire or risk collision at high speed? And why, even after they stopped the station wagon, didn't Schwerner, Goodman, and Chaney leap out and run across fields and through woods for their lives? All three were young and athletic. Even had they been fired at with shotguns, they would have had a reasonable chance to escape. Why didn't they run?

"I can understand why they didn't run," Rita said. "If Chaney was driving, or even Mickey, perhaps they did accelerate the car impulsively when they first heard the siren and saw the red light flashing. Then Mickey would have had a moment to think. He would have realized he was breaking a law in resisting an officer: the last thing he wanted to do in Mississippi. If Chaney was driving he would have said to him: 'Don't panic! Don't panic!' Andy Goodman, since he was so new down there, may have said nothing. And I think Mickey would then have decided to stop the car for the same reason he left the jail. If he defied the police, he gave them cause to shoot. If, after the station wagon was stopped, the three of them ran, they invited gunfire, perhaps bloodhounds. I think Mickey reasoned that the best hope was still to do what the police said. As a social worker in New York, he had counseled many an adolescent to try to come to terms with the police. With his whole background and training, how else could Mickey Schwerner have acted except to cooperate with the police? And even then, with a siren screaming and a red light flashing, how could Mickey have guessed that by following a police order he would lose his life?"

I have read Hannah Arendt's bitter charges that European Jews "cooperated" at Auschwitz . . . that they did not fiercely resist their murderers . . . that they chose to "let innocence be their defense" . . . that they marched like sheep to the ovens. After reflecting on what to me seems like strangely cooperative conduct by Mickey Schwerner, I asked Rita if she thought Mickey and Andy Goodman, with their belief in nonviolence, had acted to any degree like Miss Arendt says the European Jews acted.

"Not at all," Rita said. "There was nothing masochistic about Mickey. He wanted to live: he loved life. He didn't want to die. He was as capable of fear as any young man. I have seen him afraid. It's true that he didn't fear a few days in jail. And he had no great fear of being slapped, kicked, or beaten. But to save his life, I think he would have done anything within his physical power. It's just that, even after all our talk of danger, Mickey Schwerner was incapable of believing that a police officer in the United States would arrest him on a highway for the purpose of murdering him, then and there, in the dark."

That, I suppose, must be the answer. It leaves me with this melancholy thought. James Chaney's instinct to run from a police car might have saved three lives. But Chaney's simpler instinct apparently was overruled by Schwerner's reasoned and civilized judgment. So maybe Chaney's devotion to Schwerner cost him his life. Or maybe Schwerner, by taking Chaney to his death, gave meaning to Chaney's life.

• • •

When the three were ordered or pulled from the station wagon, I think they must have been placed in handcuffs, though I was told that they were not. "They were still following orders," I was told, "and Schwerner and Goodman still didn't think they were going to be killed. They thought they were going to be whipped."

I was told that James Chaney recognized one of the men from Meridian, called him by name, and asked him for help.

The murder was done in the "cut" on Rock Cut Road, less than a mile from Highway 19, about four miles from where the three were taken from the station wagon. It was before midnight, and the moon was still high. Three cars were in the cut. I was told that the three victims said nothing, but that they were jeered by the murderers. Several of the murderers chanted in unison, as though they had practiced it:

"Ashes to ashes, Dust to dust, If you'd stayed where you belonged, You wouldn't be here with us."

Another said: "So you wanted to come to Mississippi? Well, now we're gonna let you stay here. We're not even gonna run you out. We're gonna let you stay here with us."

When Schwerner was pulled from the car and stood up to be shot, I was told that the man with the pistol asked him: "You still think a nigger's as good as I am?" No time was allowed for a reply. He was shot straight through the heart and fell to the ground.

Goodman was next, with nothing said. Apparently he stood as still as Schwerner did, facing his executioner, for the shot that killed him was the same precise shot. I was told that another man fired the shot, using the same pistol, but my

opinion remains that one man fired both shots. I also still believe that both Schwerner and Goodman were in handcuffs,
and that the cuffs were removed after they were dead.

Chaney was last, and the only difference was that he strug-
gled while the others had not. He didn't stand still; he tried to
pull and duck away from his executioner. So he wasn't shot
with the same precision, and he was shot three times instead
of once.

Because Chaney's wrist, shoulder, and skull were crushed,
a reputable New York doctor who examined Chaney's body
said that he had been beaten, perhaps with a chain. Certainly
the murderers were capable of it: they were capable of anything. But I would guess that it didn't happen, though he certainly could have been badly hurt in the struggle. All three
bodies were buried in darkness with a bulldozer. They were
also uncovered, forty-four days later, with a bulldozer. The
bulldozers could easily have done additional bone damage to
Chaney.

The federal indictment concerned with these murders
charges that the three were let out of jail about 10:30 P.M.,
and that they were murdered on June 21, 1964. This means
that federal agents are convinced that the murder was done
before midnight. So these murders were committed with dis-
patch. There was no horsing around, or "interrogation," or
torture, as in the case of Edward Aaron. When white-supremacy terrorists are bent on murder they seldom pause to torture. And they usually hate "nigger-lovers" more than they
hate "niggers." Which is why I think that—if they were going
to single out a victim and beat him—Schwerner, not Chaney,
would have been the preferred choice.

*This report of the action at the murder scene has proved
accurate. In the final chapter I will again describe this action,
as best it can legally be described, in the light of testimony at
the trial.*

The three bodies were tossed into the station wagon and
driven along dirt roads to a farm about six miles southwest of
Philadelphia. A "cattle pond" was under construction on this
farm. There are scores of such ponds in Neshoba County. A
pond is created by erecting an earthen dam in a proper spot.
To begin building a dam you generally dig a ditch maybe 30
feet wide and 5 feet deep and 100 or more feet long. Into
this ditch you pack red clay; it hardens, and creates a base
for the dam under which water will not seep. Onto this base
you then pile dirt, sloping the sides, to whatever height is

needed. You plant grass along the sides. A finished dam may be 30 feet wide at the base, 10 feet wide at the top, 20 feet high, and 100 feet long, all erected on the red-clay base.

Such a dam is a perfect place in which to hide bodies. On June 21 only the red-clay base had been built, and a bulldozer was parked at the scene. One of the conspirators operated the bulldozer. He was supposed to be waiting for the murderers, but he was late. They arrived before he did, and they had to wait almost two hours for him. The moon went down behind the trees. This wait must have been unpleasant, even for such patriots proud of their courage, and I was told that a gallon of corn whiskey was delivered to them to help them through their bloody wake. Many good stories must have been told, to cackling and thigh-slapping, during that two hours of drinking and waiting at a lonely construction site.

During the second world war I remember seeing dead soldiers buried temporarily with bulldozers. We did this at Omaha Beach. Many Americans saw this done, and I suspect it was one such old veteran who thought of playing hide-and-seek with the agents of the United States by burying these bodies with a bulldozer.

When the bulldozer operator arrived, he dug a trench in the red clay along the length of the dam. The bodies, fully clothed, were tossed into this trench, face down, side by side. Goodman and Schwerner were head to head and feet to feet; Chaney, on the outside, was in the opposite position: his feet were at Schwerner's head. The two white men's arms were above their heads, indicating that they were dropped into the dirt by one man holding wrists and another holding ankles. Chaney's arms were at his sides, probably because his wrist was broken, so he would have been carried or dragged by his armpits. The bodies were then covered with two feet of dirt, and in subsequent weeks the dam was built to a height of eighteen feet. Heavy rains fell during July; so by August first the dam was massive and grassed over—a permanent tomb for three bodies if nobody ever talked.

After the burial the station wagon was driven to a point fifteen miles northeast of Philadelphia, to the edge of the Bogue Chitto swamp. There it was doused with Diesel fuel and burned. The murderers thought this was clever, almost as clever as burying the bodies in the dam. They knew that only federal agents—no one else—would ever search for the bodies; so each move they made was part of a fascinating game they thought they were playing with the FBI.

Traditionally in race murders bodies have been thrown

into rivers and swamps in Mississippi. So the murderers, by burning the station wagon on the edge of Bogue Chitto swamp, were leading the "federals" to begin by dragging the rivers and swamps. And the murderers thought this was funny because it was hot summertime and the swamps and rivers were teeming with snakes, chiggers, and mosquitoes.

"It tickles the hell out of me," one of the murderers said, "just to think of old J. Edgar's boys sweatin' out there in that swamp, with all them chiggers, water moccasins and skeeters."

Since the bodies were buried six miles *southwest* of Philadelphia, and the station wagon was burned fifteen miles *northeast* of Philadelphia, this meant that the search would begin twenty-one miles from where the bodies were; and by the time all the rivers and swamps were searched, the dam would be completed and grassed over.

Shortly before the early dawn, the murderers had finished all their chores tidily, and the last group of them gathered on the courthouse square in Philadelphia to shake hands and congratulate one another. They all had been drinking though none could be called drunk. There they were met by an official of the state of Mississippi.

"Well, boys," he said, "you've done a good job. You've struck a blow for the White Man. Mississippi can be proud of you. You've let these agitatin' Outsiders know where this state stands. Go home now and forget it. But before you go, I'm looking each one of you in the eye and telling you this: the first man who talks is *dead!* If anybody who knows anything about this ever opens his mouth to any Outsider about it, then the rest of us are going to kill him just as dead as we killed those three sonsofbitches tonight.

"Does everybody understand what I'm saying? The man who talks is dead . . . dead . . . *dead!*"

NINE

If I live to be a hundred, I'll never forget the attitudes I encountered, the stories I heard and read, and the sensations I felt in Mississippi during the last week in June and the weeks of July 1964. The *Clarion-Ledger* of Jackson calls itself Mississippi's Leading Newspaper for More Than a Century. On June 30 the *Clarion* adorned its front page with four pictures from Philadelphia. One picture showed old men dozing on the courthouse porch, and another showed Cecil Price and four highway patrol officers sprawled in lounge chairs "in conference" under shade trees. Here is the accompanying story:

LIFE GOES ON MUCH AS BEFORE
AT PHILADELPHIA DESPITE EVENTS

A week ago last Monday, Philadelphia was just another typical Mississippi town. The sun rose as usual and there were chores to be done.

A week ago last Monday people in these parts were preparing for the coming work week. Pulpwood trucks began their treck [*sic*] to the forests, store owners were busy sweeping out, the old men began moving to their usual places on the steps of the brick courthouse in the middle of the business district which forms a square.

A week ago diesel trucks braked to a halt on the main highway which runs in front of the courthouse. A few Choctaw Indians had arrived in town early for shopping. A group of young boys skipped down the street thinking about a swim later in the day.

A week ago the main problem facing Philadelphians was the coming Neshoba County Fair. And for Philadelphians, and others, that wasn't really a problem.

A week ago there was some talk around the courthouse

122

about three so-called civil rights workers being arrested for speeding. After they had posted bail, a deputy sheriff had followed them part of the way back to Meridian. The old men, long experts of the courthouse talk, first heard from local officials of the three having disappeared.

A week ago that was not much to get excited about. The trio [were] unknown locally, and who knew which way they might have gone when they left Philadelphia?

Then Monday afternoon a burned station wagon, used by the three, was found about 12 miles northeast of town. Since that time Philadelphia has led most news stories all over the world.

During the past seven days, Neshoba Countians have seen hundreds of federal agents, highway patrol personnel, and even members of the U.S. Navy trampling over the countryside. They have heard the President of the United States talk about their town. They have read about a visit by Allen Dulles to Mississippi to discuss their town. They have seen one of the largest groups of news media personnel ever to gather in Mississippi. They have seen their town Philadelphia, through the eyes of national television; they have heard about their town on radio; they have seen their town through the "eyes" of newsprint and pictures.

They have seen their town tried and found guilty by many outsiders . . . an observer can hear phrases of displeasure, particularly concerning national television personnel who have . . . attempted to outdo each other. . . .

An observer . . . immediately gets the feeling that Philadelphians would rather just be left alone. "If people would 'tend to their own business, everything would be alright," one old courthouse sitter said.

"If it was boiled down to gravy there wouldn't be much to it, nohow," another responded.

An inquirer gets the feeling that these Mississippians don't know what happened to the three. And after the treatment they have received from national news media, they wouldn't care to cooperate with visiting television folk.

Monday afternoon was like most Monday afternoons have been in Philadelphia for years. And Philadelphia will be here for many more Mondays to come.

On July 2 the Birmingham *News,* which has a large circulation in east Mississippi, published this Editorial Report on its editorial page:

The Scene: Philadelphia

Four hundred sailors, scores of FBI agents—employees of Uncle Sam—push through dust, weeds, branches, mud and water not far from this national dateline. Eleven hours a day they hunt for clues of three missing men.

Few Mississippians, officials or otherwise, seem to be doing very much active searching.

A Mississippi highway patrolman accompanies each squad of sailors. Their mission, said Gov. Paul Johnson, is to "be certain that the people's houses and property of this area are protected at all times."

Some state investigators, including some brass, spend a good portion of every day under a giant pecan tree behind the small Philadelphia City Hall.

One top investigator, pistol on, lies stretched out in an aluminum, web lounge chair, arms up behind his head. Four or five other chairs under the sheltering tree are for other state men who come and go. . . .

State people for the most part seem to be standing by. Federal agents carry the burden of effort to find the missing men.

It is a distinctly pleasant sort of Southern scene—state investigators behind City Hall eat lunch calmly—sardines, cheese, crackers, dill pickles, cold sweet milk. Sometimes there is baloney and souse meat.

Last Tuesday morning several highway patrol cars stood parked near a church to the west. Maybe more such are present than are needed. These officers only stood around talking to each other. "We were just told to park here," said one.

The Philadelphia police chief and his assistants haven't been evident much in the searching either. Most of the time they seem busy about their duties in town. . . .

The police chief and Philadelphia's mayor provided a small courtroom for state and federal officers, for private phone calls and conferences. Meetings between federal and state men have been increasingly few recently.

The FBI, quite obviously, is keeping almost strictly to itself. Its information is close-guarded. State men give no evidence that federal agents tell them much when they do sit down together.

There is a careful courtesy between local and state officers and federal investigators. But there is an obvious distance between them too. State people appear to feel that the FBI ought to be confiding more in them. Equally apparent, the FBI—which usually says as little as possible—seems to feel its facts are best kept to itself. "Cooperation" in Neshoba County is more ritual than reality.

Gov. Johnson of Mississippi has said, "this [search] is a joint effort. This is a cooperative effort between local, state and federal agents. . . ."

The federal agents do not mix. They attend to their business and mind their tongues. They are quartered in a small motel due west of Philadelphia. They do not tarry long at City Hall when they must visit it.

Monday a federal agent pulled his car up to park near City Hall. His vehicle blocked a woman clerk's car as she worked inside.

A state man suggested someone ought to tell the agent, so he could move his car.

"Wait until he's walked up here," said another state officer under the pecan tree.

"This is a cooperative effort," the governor had said.

How could such officers cooperate in the search for the bodies? Not every state officer knew where the bodies were, but some undoubtedly did and those who didn't probably assumed that other officers did know. A sheriff is a state as well as a county officer; so is his deputy. The Governor of Mississippi can arrest a sheriff, investigate him, replace him. If there was a state police officer assigned to the search who doubted that Sheriff Rainey knew where the bodies were, I didn't meet him. And if there was a state police officer who doubted that Deputy Price had been party to the murders, I didn't meet him either.

How could the FBI cooperate with Sheriff Rainey, Deputy Price, and other state officers who sympathized with the murderers? The FBI represents the free society of the United States. The state officers represent the white-supremacy society of Mississippi. No free society can approve murder, or lynching, or cop-inflicted punishment. Every white-supremacy society tolerates "extremism in its own defense." Mississippi, in effect, approved lynching for decades, as it has approved a hundred cases where "troublemakers" were shot "while resisting arrest."

Since white supremacy cannot now be maintained legally within the United States, how else is it to be maintained except by resort to illegality whenever it feels threatened?

With passage of the Civil Rights Act of 1964, the free society of the United States moved into another showdown with the white-supremacy society of Mississippi. Just as in 1861, when freedom came to a showdown with slavery. This is why the murders were committed: the white-supremacy society trying to protect itself from Invaders it could not repel legally.

How could the "outside press"—the free press of the United States—have pleased the people of Philadelphia? Murder had been committed. The victims were innocent: they were in Mississippi legally and deserved the protection of Mississippi's laws. So the free press felt the bodies should be found and the murderers should be tracked down and punished.

To most, if not all, of the people of Philadelphia no murder had been committed. If killing had been done, it was because the victims had "provoked" the killers. How can killing be called murder "when the victims have come in from the outside just to stir up trouble"? Most of the people of Philadelphia did not want the bodies to be found, and they stood ready to protect and reward the killers.

"Sheriff Rainey is the bravest sheriff in America," announced Circuit Judge O. H. Barnett. Does a sheriff prove he is brave by conspiring to murder three helpless young men, who have broken no law, and who are armed only with opinions the sheriff happens to detest? That is what the federal grand jury indictment, referred to previously, says Sheriff Rainey did. Judge Barnett is another duly elected Mississippi agent, the judge who would charge any state grand jury investigating the case, and the judge who would preside at any Neshoba County trial of the murderers. At a meeting of the State Sheriffs Association, Sheriff Rainey was the hero, "applauded to the rafters."

The only way the national press could have pleased the people of Neshoba County would have been to insist that Sheriff Rainey or Deputy Price, rather than Martin Luther King, deserved the Nobel Peace Prize, and to publish a series of articles or produce a television special proving that Mickey Schwerner and Andy Goodman had been Soviet spies sent to "mongrelize Mississippi."

The FBI could have pleased the people of Mississippi only by respecting that mudsill of white supremacy, states' rights (racist version), and by reporting to and working with Sheriff Rainey and Deputy Price.

In an effort to pretend that cooperation existed between Mississippi and the national press, the Mississippi State Highway Patrol established a press headquarters at the Benwalt Hotel in Philadelphia. Telephones were installed for the visiting press, and a personable young man presented himself as the press representative for the state police. He invited me to attend briefings and use the facilities. I declined with thanks.

Hypocrisy sometimes makes me physically ill. I respect several officers in the Mississippi patrol. They are fine and capable men. They don't like the Ku Klux Klan, and they wouldn't give Lawrence Rainey or Cecil Price the time of day. If they had really been in a position to work on this case, they might have needed an entire afternoon to find those bodies and arrest the first score of these murderers. I'm sure those good men felt embarrassed by the position they were in. Let's just say that the Mississippi state police have done proud work before, and may do proud work again. But not in this case. Here they could accomplish nothing. Because what we had here was a lynching, with police participation.

· · ·

After the murder, in their treatment of Rita Schwerner the people of Mississippi had to try to degrade her. To risk showing her any sympathy would be to risk showing respect for her murdered husband. Besides, she had slept in "nigger houses."

Asleep in a dormitory in Oxford, Ohio, Rita was awakened about 1 A.M. on Monday morning and asked to come to the office of the Western College for Women. At the office she took the telephone call from Jackson and learned that the three were missing and presumed to be in jail somewhere in Mississippi. She lay on a cot for the rest of the night, taking telephone calls. Sometime after daylight she learned that Neshoba county jail now reported that the three had been detained there during Sunday evening and released at 10:30 P.M. So the three were now said to be "missing."

Rita spent Monday in Oxford, and on Tuesday morning some students drove her the sixty miles to the Cincinnati Airport. There she learned that the burned car had been found.

· · ·

"I knew then that they were dead," she told me. "I took a plane to Atlanta where I had to spend the night in a motel in order to make the connection to Meridian."

She reached Meridian on Wednesday, and FBI agents questioned her for three hours. Then on Thursday, the twenty-fifth, with a lawyer, she drove to Philadelphia to see Sheriff Rainey. The sheriff ducked her at first; then, accompanied by a highway patrol investigator, Charles Snodgrass, he agreed to talk with her while sitting in his car at the Delphia Motel. Rainey sat under the wheel; Snodgrass was at his right; and Rita and her lawyer sat in the back seat for perhaps ten minutes. Snodgrass insisted on doing most of the talking.

"Mrs. Schwerner, you mustn't be hard on Sheriff Rainey," Snodgrass said. "He's a worried husband. His wife is in the hospital. He's preoccupied, and he knows very little about this case."

"Well, at least he still has a wife to be concerned about,"

Rita said. "I ask him only to do me the courtesy of telling me where my husband is."

"But the sheriff doesn't know that," Snodgrass insisted. "He was at the hospital with his wife. How can the sheriff know where your husband decided to go when he left Philadelphia Sunday night?"

Rita persisted in trying to address the sheriff directly. She said: "Sheriff Rainey, I feel that you know what happened. I'm going to find out if I can. If you don't want me to find out, you'll have to kill me."

Rainey's huge knuckles turned white as he tightened his grip on the steering wheel. "I'm very shocked," he said. "I'm sorry you said that."

From Philadelphia Rita went on to Jackson to try to see Governor Johnson. But she waited at the governor's office in vain because he was preoccupied in greeting George Wallace and in helping Wallace address a "mammoth mass meeting" on Thursday evening. "I'm sure Wallace is much more important to Mississippi than three missing men," Rita told reporters at the governor's office.

On Friday every front page in Mississippi carried a three-or four-column cut of Wallace and Johnson "in triumph." Here, in part, is the UPI story as it appeared in the Meridian *Star*:

Gov. Johnson Sides with 'Bama Chief

SOUTH WILL NAME NEXT PRESIDENT,
WALLACE TELLS 10,000 IN JACKSON

Jackson, Miss.—Gov. George Wallace of Alabama was backed up by Mississippi Gov. Paul Johnson here Thursday night in telling a roaring crowd of 10,000 that "the South will determine who is the next president of the United States."

Wallace and his wife spent the afternoon as guests at the executive mansion before the Alabama governor addressed the boisterous turnout of Mississippians at the State Coliseum.

"Certainly I am a candidate for president," Wallace said. "I am running for president because I was born free. I want your children and mine and our posterity to be unencumbered by the manipulations of a soulless state."

Johnson introduced the Alabama governor, assuring the crowd that "the South, with its 112 electoral votes, is the balance of power that will determine who is the next president of the United States."

"It's time the white people of our various states started bloc voting," said Johnson.

Wallace predicted at a news conference earlier in the day that Mississippi would follow the lead of his native state and pledge its electoral votes to him.

"No president of this nation will be elected unless he pays attention to Mississippi and Alabama," he said. "The people are tired of being taken for granted and kicked around by the leaders of both national parties."

Young couples carrying infants and adults leading elderly parents by the arm turned out to hear Wallace's plea for presidential support. They swarmed the speaker's s[t]and at the conclusion of the speech to touch the Alabamian's outstretched arms.

Police estimated the crowd at more than 10,000—possibly the largest throng since the coliseum was built two years ago. A Dixieland band, dancing girls, and "We Love George" cries caused one native of Alabama to remark: "They don't even do this in Alabama. . . ."

Gov. Johnson sided with Wallace in saying "the South has no use for the liberals of either . . . national parties. We want a choice—not of two liberals—but a clear cut choice between a liberal and a conservative. . . ."

Wallace called the 1954 school desegregation ruling by the U.S. Supreme Court "ridiculous and asinine," and said "any person who made such a ruling should have a psychiatric examination. . . ." The Governor noted that the National Press Club presented speakers' certificates to Nikita Khrushchev and Fidel Castro but refused him such a certificate.

The crowd roared when he said: "As far as I'm concerned, they can take their certificate, and you know what they can do with it."

White supremacists like Wallace, Barnett, and Johnson are always repeating the lie that they represent "the South." They long ago captured the term *states' rights,* and in 1964 they tried to capture the word *conservative.* They began implying that all Southerners and all Americans who think of themselves as conservative, or who value the rights of the states, are also white supremacists.

Since Wallace was the Presidential candidate of the white-supremacy terrorists, among the ten thousand who roared for him at Jackson were at least fifty men who knew of the plot to murder Mickey Schwerner and three men who were members of the murder party. When neither Wallace nor Johnson mentioned the disappearance of Schwerner, Chaney and Goodman, every conspirator and murderer left the Coliseum feeling that he had the approval of both Wallace and Johnson.

Here is another UPI story out of Jackson, as carried by the Meridian *Star* June 26.

COULD HAPPEN ANYWHERE,
GOVERNOR SAYS

Gov. Paul Johnson said today he was "satisfied" that everything possible was being done to locate the three civil rights workers missing since earlier this week in East-Central Mississippi.

Johnson told newsmen the disappearance of the three was something that "could happen anytime" in any part of the country. "It happens in New York every night," he said, adding that Misssissippi has the second lowest crime rate in the nation.

"I'm satisfied that everything is being done that could be done to find them," he said.

Johnson also acknowledged that a second wave of volunteer workers, mostly college students, was expected to arrive in Mississippi during the weekend to participate in the so-called "summer project."

But he said he understood the number may have decreased from earlier expectations. He said he had heard reports that a number of the students had decided against taking part in the project, some on their own and some because of their parents.

The governor was ignoring the characteristics which set the Philadelphia murders apart. The murders committed "nightly" in New York are not the result of plans in which the police have participated. They are not widely approved by the people, and the state seeks to punish the murderers. The governor was failing to note that few Mississippians were extending themselves in the search for the bodies. And by reporting that the number of students coming to Mississippi "may have decreased from earlier expectations," the governor, in effect, was informing the murderers that their action was proving effective.

At the trial in Meridian I was told by a Klansman: "Most every man involved in this killing still believes, and knows down deep in his heart, that he helped save Mississippi. If that killing hadn't been done when it was, then thousands more of them kooks and Commies would'a come streaming into this state. The killing turned 'em back."

Rita Schwerner found Governor Johnson Friday afternoon on the steps of the governor's mansion. He and Wallace were still receiving well-wishers, and Rita walked up to meet him, He didn't catch her name at first, so he smiled and extended his hand as though she were a constituent. A highway patrolman shouted a warning, repeating her name, and the governor jerked back his hand and fled, with Wallace, into the house and slammed the door.

"Johnson and Wallace reminded me of two scared children," Rita said. "They stood peeping at me from behind curtains, as though they were curious about me but feared to be seen in public with me."

Not until July 30, in a courtroom in Hattiesburg, did Rita corner Deputy Price. She walked up to him, extended her hand, and said: "I'd like to say hello to you, Mr. Price." He literally jumped away from her and stood gritting his teeth at her. "I don't want to talk to you!" he said in a strangely nervous, high-pitched voice.

For two brave law-enforcement officers, Rainey and Price seemed unduly reluctant to confront the ninety-pound Mrs. Schwerner.

When Rita left the courtroom in Hattiesburg, she found a crowd waiting on the courthouse steps for her. The crowd began jeering as she approached.

"Smell her!" one woman shouted.

"You can actually smell her!" others shouted.

"She stinks!"

Rita walked on down the steps, followed by the calls that she "smelled" and "stank."

As the search moved into its third and fourth weeks, the entire Mississippi press began emphasizing how the civil rights workers "smelled" and "stank." Here is part of another story from the *Clarion-Ledger:*

ODOR OF SWEAT, DIRT FILLS
HATTIESBURG'S COFO OFFICE

Walk into the grey-concrete office of the Council of Federated Organizations at 507 Mobile St. in Hattisburg [and] the first thing noticed is the odor of sweat and dirt. . . .

Perhaps a dozen Negroes and half a dozen whites meet you at the door to ask your business. The Negroes, as the whites, are poorly dressed. Two white girls with long, straight hair . . . sandals and sack dresses stand by a desk, idly eyeing the intruder.

The appearance of the COFO workers is an affront to

most of Hattiesburg's residents . . . a 1964 graduate of the University of Southern Mississippi summed it up like this: "If you don't know them . . . by sight, you could sniff the air and find out."

A police officer, working the Mobile Street beat, tabbed the group, "disgusting, just plain disgusting."

The office, from which is controlled COFO's mission to southeast Mississippi, consists of two small rooms and dingy kitchen. A roach scuttles across the floor. A Negro boy—perhaps 18—steps on it with a crackling sound, smiles . . . and says, "Our friends."

A white youth wearing torn blue-jeans, a work shirt and tennis shoes, sits in a corner plucking away tunelessly at a beat-down guitar.

There is much talk about Mississippi as a police state, the cold "brutality" of the people and the superior intelligence of the COFO workers.

COFO's project director, Sanford Leigh of Illinois, is 28 years old and claims to have been in Mississippi since 1961. He is a darker-than-usual Negro, very thin, with black rimmed glasses and a way of looking at his knees when he speaks.

Leigh, who is a college graduate, does most of the group's talking [and is] belligerent.

"Nigger, nigger, nigger, that's what you think while you're standing there," he said. "Just another of the state's yellow journalists working for the state's most condemnatory paper."

Leigh likes the word "condemnatory." He uses it over and over.

[Another spokesman for the group is a white native of Connecticut, Class of '66 at Duke. Tall and rangy, he looks like a beatnik, complete with torn sandals.]

"I'm not down here to impress you or anybody," he said. "If I was, I'd get an ivy-league haircut and some . . . clothes. I don't need . . . clothes to make people realize I'm a human being."

[He] holds hands with a Negro girl. She wears a pin bearing the legend "Student Non-Violent Coordinating Committee —One Man, One Vote." After a while, [he] becomes angry with the . . . reporter, and he and the girl walk out to a car with New York license plates and drive away. Several police officers watch them and jot down the car's license plate.

The white workers, including the girls, live with Negroes in Hattiesburg's Negro section. They say the Negro groups furnish food but not money. COFO pays its workers $9.66 per week after taxes.

The girls spend some of their money on candy bars; the boys spend some of theirs at Negro taverns, drinking beer.

About 20 people work out of the Hattiesburg office. Half are whites. None of the white workers is from Mississippi, and none is old enough to vote.

"We don't need to vote ourselves in order to show others," one said. He was 17, a college freshman.

Because *Life* magazine, in preparing its story on the training at Oxford, Ohio, had photographed Andrew Goodman; and because film footage had been shot by CBS of Goodman at Oxford, an incredible number of Mississippians concluded that a plot had existed for Goodman to come to Mississippi and "become missing." Here is one of many letters to the editor charging a plot that were published:

After watching Walter Cronkite's super-colossal, hate Mississippi newscast, I cannot remain silent. What an array of personalities were presented to jerk tears, play upon emotions, and engender hatred for Mississippi. . . .

However, the master minds seemed to have slipped up a bit and I challenge you to ask this one question. If the planners didn't know prior to Sunday, June 21st, that Andy Goodman was going to "disappear" in Mississippi, then why did the TV cameraman who made pictures at the school in Oxford, Ohio, keep his camera on Goodman close up when there were many other students in the lecture hall with him? He was the only one they focused on and only took the camera off of him briefly to show the Negro speaker . . . telling them that violence could befall them in Mississippi. . . .

The explanation was apparent to all of us in the writing or picture business. Goodman was a particularly attractive, intelligent-looking, obviously sensitive and sincere young man, as is evident in the photo of him at Oxford reproduced in this volume from the CBS film. He was no beatnik. He was the sort that a commercial photographer spots in a crowd. Then he happened to be caught in the only plot that existed: the plot to murder Michael Schwerner.

Around the middle of July, when the search for the bodies had proceeded unsuccessfully for three weeks, I assumed that the time had come to negotiate with the murderers. The search had never had much chance of succeeding. Where such a murder has been planned; where the murderers have had many hours in which to dispose of the bodies; where there are large stretches of uninhabited countryside; and where the inhabitants are uncooperative because they are hostile to the searchers and/or afraid of the murderers, a search is largely meaningless. Under such circumstances you can't find bodies with helicopters, or with hundreds of young sailors beating bushes, killing snakes, and scratching chigger bites.

"No, we won't find anything," a federal officer said to me. "But we have to keep dragging rivers and beating the bushes while the *real* search goes on: the search for that citizen who, for protection and money, will eventually take us to the bodies."

In a murder case where every knowledgeable survivor is guilty, and where every living witness is a murderer, you obtain information from informers, and you obtain evidence by inducing one murderer to witness against another. And where every witness is under a real threat of death from his fellows if he talks, a witness can be a problem.

In this Mississippi is, in fact, no different from New York. When, because they fear involvement, thirty-eight "decent" New Yorkers neglect to call the police while an innocent woman is murdered before their eyes, how can "decent" Mississippians be expected to witness against terrorists? Bodies hidden by the Mafia and other gangsters are as hard to find as those hidden by Mississippi gangsters; and a thousand murders committed by gangsters have gone unpunished in the United States because "decent" citizens declined to take the risks of giving testimony.

. . .

I thought something might be gained by my talking with two or three secure, honorable, sophisticated men in the power structure of Philadelphia—men who were not politicians or preachers, but business or professional men, capable of some degree of objectivity, and with whom I might have mutual friends. It is well known in Mississippi that in order to publish the truth about the Emmett Till murder, I paid those murderers with the assistance of reputable alumni of the Ole Miss Law School. It is also known that in both the Mack Parker case and in the Beckwith case, I had the assistance of Mississippi lawyers and of Mississippi police investigators. For my talks with citizens of Philadelphia to be effective, the talks had to be held away from Philadelphia. I arranged such talks, which went on at some length. I thought I might persuade one of these men to assist at least in finding the bodies if not in obtaining information or evidence.

"Well," one man said, "I'll say this. I'm sorry about the murders. Of course I'm sorry. They were wrong, stupid, and very bad for business in Mississippi. I'm capable of sympathy for the victims. I'm sorry for the families. I'm sure that Schwerner and Goodman were decent, well-meaning young men. They wanted to ride white horses and, right or wrong, they were riding their horses in Mississippi. But here is a fact. On both sides everybody knew that at least one of these young people coming to Mississippi was going to be murdered. I knew it. I assume the fathers of Schwerner and Goodman knew it. I know the instigators of this 'March on Mississippi' expected at least one murder. Joe Alsop wrote that murder was expected, and that the provoking of violence was a tactic deliberately being adopted by the militant Negro organizations."

"But the fact that murder may have been expected doesn't justify it," I said.

"No, but it helps explain it. Mississippi has been a white-supremacy state since its beginning. These rednecks are capable of violence. That's why they make good soldiers; why we use them to lead night patrols in our wars; why so many of them have won Congressional Medals of Honor. They may not read much, but they now own television sets. And when they hear on TV every day that everybody in Mississippi is a stupid, tobacco-chewing bigot, then a murder case like this one here is as predictable as sunrise."

"How about helping find the bodies? For humanitarian reasons if no other?"

"Well," he said, "I'll have to think about that. I suppose I might induce one of these jokers to tell me where they are if I really set my hand to it. But what good can come of it? Maybe the best course for everybody is just to let the bodies lie and let the excitement gradually die down. Once the bodies are found, then there is a great hue and cry to convict somebody . . . to put somebody in jail. And that's a power I don't have. That power doesn't exist in Mississippi. Not even Paul Johnson has any such power. There is no way in the world, in open court, where a twelve-man jury verdict must be unanimous, and where every juror can be polled in open court and made to say how he voted—there's no possible way to ever put anybody in jail. Instead of reducing hate, all a trial can do is spread it. So why should we have all that hue and cry, and a big circus trial, with everybody goddamning Mississippi? What's the use of it? Since a murder like this was expected, why don't we all just admit that we got what we expected and devote ourselves to trying to prevent another one?"

"How do we prevent another one by letting this one go unpunished?"

"This one is going unpunished in any case. That is, the murderers are going unpunished. Mississippi has already been punished, and will continue to be punished."

"So you refuse to help find the bodies?"

"I haven't said that," he answered. "I'll have to think about it. It's a tough question. It's *right* that the bodies should be found. But nothing good can come of finding them."

"Well, here is another of your realities," I said. "The bodies *will* be found. You know it as well as I do. The pressure is great and will get greater. Too many people know where the bodies are. One of them is sure to sell out. There is too much money available."

"How much money?"

"I'd say twenty-five thousand dollars. More if necessary."

"You mean twenty-five thousand dollars for nothing more than the *information* as to where the bodies are? No confession? No public identification of the informer? No signed statement identifying and accusing the others?"

"I think that can be arranged," I said. "If all we can get is the bodies. Naturally, a signed confession which implicates the others would be best, but if we can't get that let's at least get the evidence of murder. The deal will have to be COD. Nobody will pay an informer that amount of money just for an unproved tip. The informer has to pass the information, then wait two or three days while the FBI finds the bodies and identifies them. The informer has to take the calculated risk that he will get his money, but ways can be devised to reduce the risk to a minimum."

"Christ," he said, "maybe I ought to stop what I'm doing and get in the business of finding and selling the bodies of civil rights workers."

"Well, what I'm telling you is no secret," I said. "The FBI has always paid informers. So does every effective police agency on earth. How else could these bodies ever be found? Or these murderers identified? I think the bodies will be found, and I think that many, perhaps most, of the murderers will eventually be identified even if they are never convicted."

In addition to such talks with substantial citizens of Philadelphia, I spread my Alabama and Mississippi telephone numbers around and let it be widely known that I would pay for information. The FBI agents were doing the same thing. I told them most of what I was doing. They didn't tell me what they were doing: they quite properly never tell anybody.

By July 20 I believed I knew the identity of three of the young men who were in the actual murder and burial parties. I had been told that the bodies had been buried, not submerged; and I had the information that the graves were southwest of Philadelphia. I told one of my publishers that the bodies would be found "not later than August tenth," and I wrote the first draft of a story titled *How the Bodies Were Found in Mississippi*.

I was convinced that by August eighth I would know where the bodies were; and I assumed the FBI agents were as close or closer to a deal than I was.

On July 22 U.S. Senator James O. Eastland of Mississippi made a statement I still can't understand. The Senator is an able, immensely knowledgeable, and powerful man. Not only did he practice skillful law for years in Mississippi before he went to the Senate, but in the Senate he is chairman of the powerful Judiciary Committee and deals daily with the Justice Department. Here is the press association report on his statement:

> Sen. James O. Eastland . . . suggested Wednesday that the . . . disappearance of three civil rights workers in Mississippi might have been a hoax
>
> [He questioned charges that the three had been killed.]
>
> He said an intensive, month-long investigation and search had failed to produce "a shred of evidence" that the three were victims of racial violence.
>
> "Many people in our state assert that there is just as much evidence, as of today, that they are voluntarily missing as there is that they have been abducted," said Eastland.
>
> "No one wants to charge that a hoax has been perpetrated, because there is too little evidence to show just what did happen. But as time goes on, and the search continues, if some evidence of a crime is not produced, I think the people of America will be justified in considering other alternatives more valid solutions to the mystery, instead of accepting as true the accusation of the agitators that heinous crime has been committed."
>
> He claimed that Mississippians were attempting to preserve the peace in the face of a Communist-backed "conspiracy to thrust violence upon them." . . .

Why would Senator Eastland make such a statement as late as July 22? Did the information on which he based his statement come from Governor Johnson? Or from the head of the Mississippi highway patrol? Had the state investigators actually done so little work on the case that they had found "not a shred of evidence that the three were victims of racial violence?" Had it occurred to Senator Eastland or Governor Johnson to call Sheriff Rainey before them and ask what had happened? Or was everybody in Mississippi standing back, averting his eyes, and hoping the FBI would find nothing?

On Saturday, August 1, I was told that FBI agents were guarding the dam. I was told that Deputy Price knew that the FBI had found the bodies; and I was told that FBI agents were not allowing Price near the dam. Sheriff Rainey, for some reason, had picked that week end to go on his vacation, along the Mississippi Gulf Coast.

On Monday, August 3, a federal judge in Biloxi secretly gave the FBI authority to enter the property around the dam and to excavate in the dam. The warrant was issued on the sworn statement of an FBI agent that "an informer" had provided the information that the bodies were in the dam.

On Monday night a truck and trailer left Jackson, Mississippi, carrying a bulldozer and an excavating machine known as a dragline. On Tuesday the dragline lumbered out to the center of the dam and began cutting a perfect V. Eighteen feet down, at the exact bottom of the V, the dragline and bulldozer, then FBI agents with shovels, uncovered a cruel tomb.

In a photograph published around the world—a photograph that should live—Sheriff's Deputy Cecil Price was shown helping to carry the plastic bags in which were the forty-four-day-old remains of Michael Schwerner, James Chaney, and Andrew Goodman.

TEN

For several days after the bodies were found they were kept in Jackson for autopsy. Then they were released to the families, and memorial services were held in New York, Meridian, and Longdale. These memorial services thus coincided in time with the Neshoba County Fair. It was a remarkable juxtaposition, made even more remarkable by the fact that the fairground is almost within sight of the dam from which the bodies had been excavated.

Here is how the fair is described in its official releases:

The historically famous Neshoba County Fair is the only Campground Fair in the United States. There have been others but they have long since passed from the scene. . . .

Located in a park-like setting; eight miles from Philadelphia, Mississippi; the fairground is a small city of its own; patterned after the typical Southern town, with a square but without a court house. A giant-size open air pavilion sits in the center of the "square." Cabins and houses surround the square providing residents with Campground facilities. There are more than 250 such houses—with more than 2000 patrons occupying them for the week of the fair. . . . "Mississippi's Giant Houseparty!" The cabins are owned and built by the individual families. Many are maintained by those who have moved away years ago but make the annual pilgrimage back home for the fair. . . .

Annual entertainment features include: Beauty Pageant; the exhibits; two great livestock shows; daily harness . . . races; grandstand shows; and an array of events presented at the open air pavilion. [But the fair is also called] "The Political Battleground of Mississippi." All prominent officeholders, political aspirants on the national and state levels, consider the fair a "must."

. . . Western bands have a picnic; "Grand Ole Opry stars" have been coming for years; and there are "Rock 'n' Roll and

139

Pop" for the Teeners. . . . The red clay track of Neshoba
County Fair has held more annual licensed meets than any
track in the deep south. . . .

Nothing is left undone to provide a full week of entertainment—for young and old. No place is as exciting and different. For fundamental lovers of an old form of Americana
—if you love "folks" and want to go back to your "raising,"
this historically famous Neshoba County Campground Fair is
the place to go.

The fair therefore was Mississippi's largest and oldest Summer Festival. Politics was one of its forms of amusement.
Since 1964 was a Presidential year, Presidential politics was
on everybody's mind. Since Mississippi is a one-party state,
there is never any contest over whom the state will support
for President. In 1964 "everybody" was for Goldwater. Because they thought Goldwater was "against civil rights." And
because they mistakenly thought Goldwater had shouted:
"Murder in defense of white supremacy is no vice." The principal speaker at the fair was to be Barry Goldwater, Jr. The
second principal speaker was to be George Wallace. And
Ross Barnett would "warm up the crowd" for both of the visitors. So they thought the fair would be one long shout of
defiance of the United States.

Here is a second press report:

HOUSEPARTIES CLASSIC PART
OF WEEK-LONG ACTIVITIES

Philadelphia, Miss.—It's a classic—the Neshoba County Fair
—the only one of its kind.

The official fair opening is tomorrow, but for this . . . city
thrown into the national news spotlight with a triple civil
rights slaying, the fair has been underway for over a month.

For the real fair . . . is the house party. . . .

The latter is sort of an old camp meeting, family and community reunion, hootenanny, picnic, fellowship meeting and
vacation outing all thrown into one week of . . . leisurely
country living. People here enjoy it . . . they love it. It is the
one big event they all look forward to the year around . . .

About 2500 persons are expected to "move in" for the fair.

Families . . . own cabins—most are two-storied, but some
of the earliest built are one-story. . . .

Many of the cabins are unpainted, many are painted
brightly. Most were built by their owners. . . .

The fair begins annually in early August. But as early as
late June "fair families" are cleaning cabins and beginning to

move in. Usually they move in a week before the fair actually opens. . . .

. . . cabins provide a base of operations for the colorful all-day and all-night houseparty gaiety. Occupants mingle freely in a union of close fellowship throughout fair week. It is not unusual for the fairgoers to sing almost until dawn. . . .

"Ya'all come to Mississippi's Giant Houseparty."

Early fairgoers were annoyed by the roadblocks FBI agents maintained around the area where the bodies had been found. Here is the UPI report from Philadelphia on August 7:

Townsfolk were determined today that the annual county fair would help ease tensions in this East Mississippi area where the bodies of three civil rights workers were found early in the week. . . .

The fairgrounds, where carnival workers . . . are busy setting up rides and . . . games of chance, is only two miles south of the sand dam where the bodies were uncovered late Tuesday.

FBI experts were combing the area for additional clues, painstakingly sifting the soil through a big screen mounted on two wooden sawhorses.

Early fairgoers had to drive past roadblocks leading down gravel roads to the scene of the intense investigation. . . .

The main highlight will come Thursday when almost every state official is expected to be on hand for traditional political speeches. Among those scheduled to appear this year are Alabama Gov. George Wallace, former Mississippi Gov. Ross Barnett and possibly Barry Goldwater, Jr.

But young Goldwater didn't show. The star disappointed his audience. Perhaps someone told him that Negroes attend the Giant Houseparty only as servants in those cabins of good fellowship. Or perhaps he realized that he might feel uncomfortable supporting states' rights within sight of that demolished dam, and saying that law enforcement in Mississippi should be left to sheriffs and highway patrolmen. Young Goldwater was to have spoken on Thursday, August 13. But on August 11 the fairgoers were told that there had been a mixup in scheduling and that the young man couldn't make it.

Then even Wallace chickened out. He decided that an appearance might not help even his image. So in a Presidential year no Presidential aspirants appeared. Governor Johnson had to come to the fair and fill in for Wallace. A Jackson physician, Dr. Ney Williams, filled in for young Goldwater.

Dr. Williams told "a cheering crowd of 6000 persons" that "the FBI ought to be out hunting Communists instead of civil rights workers in Mississippi." He said he wanted to get Communists out of the federal government, impeach Chief Justice Earl Warren, eliminate foreign aid, and get the United States out of the United Nations.

A dozen lesser Mississippi politicians helped warm up the crowd, chiefly with the shout: "I have lost all respect for the National Council of Churches!" Barnett told the jokes: all the funny ones how Mr. Clean could help the dirty, filthy, stinking civil rights workers; and about the President's theme song being "The High Yellow Rose of Texas."

Reporting Governor Johnson's speech, the *Clarion-Ledger* began:

> Gov. Paul B. Johnson told a cheering crowd of some 6000 persons at the Neshoba County Fair here Wednesday afternoon that neither Mississippians nor their state and county officers have any obligation to enforce the federal civil rights law.
>
> "You can't drive the people of Mississippi any time nor any where," the state's chief executive declared.
>
> "Integration is like prohibition," Johnson explained, "if people don't want it a whole army can't enforce it. People who want to enforce integration in Mississippi had better think 900,000 times."
>
> Continuing, Gov. Johnson emphasized that "segregation is the only way to peace and harmony between the races."

Governor Johnson told the crowd that one of the nation's problems was "the delinquency of adults who ignore their children, like those delinquent adults who allowed their children to invade Mississippi this summer." He said: "The white people of Mississippi know that the vast majority of the colored people of this state have turned their backs on the motley crew of invaders of our state. We will not permit outsiders to subvert our people and our rights."

The governor finally took note of the open grave which was almost within his sight. "The people of Neshoba County are law-abiding people," he said. "Some news media have tried hard to run down this section of our state. They jump on an isolated incident, but ignore 804 unsolved cases of murder and missing persons in the state of New York."

In all the words shouted at the Neshoba County Fair there was not one word of sympathy for the victims and not one word of blame for the murderers. If you can't blame, you can't punish. A criminal who is not blamed feels approved. In the crowd that cheered Governor Johnson there must have been at least a hundred men who had what the law calls "prior knowledge" of the plot to murder Mickey Schwerner, and at least eight men who were in the murder and burial parties.

Every one of those conspirators and murderers left the fair convinced that he enjoyed the approval of his governor and of "all the decent people in Mississippi."

   . . .

While the thousands were preparing to celebrate their "giant houseparty" at the Neshoba County Fair, a few miles away, in Meridian, James Chaney was buried. Here is a partial press account:

> Slain Negro civil rights worker James Chaney was buried here Friday in a quiet—almost secret—service. . . .
>
> Within an hour of the time Chaney's body was returned to Meridian from the University of Mississippi Medical Center in Jackson it was buried in a newly constructed hilltop cemetery southwest of Meridian, with his immediate family, a few close friends and several civil rights workers present. . . .
>
> Chaney's body is only the second to be buried in the Memorial Park cemetery atop Mt. Barton, just off Valley Road.
>
> The body arrived here at 5 P.M. and was taken to a Negro funeral home.
>
> There were less than 15 mourners and no flowers at the cemetery when an old black hearse climbed the red-clay hill to the new burying ground. The short funeral cortege was led by a Lauderdale County deputy sheriff and a Meridian Police Department Negro patrolman. . . .
>
> Four Negro men carried Chaney's gray casket from the hearse to the grave. In the gathering darkness a six-minute funeral service was conducted by Rev. William Hervey, of Brunswick, New Jersey. The coffin was then placed in a gold-painted concrete vault and lowered into the grave.
>
> A crowd of about 25 newsmen and photographers watched from a distance.

Rita Schwerner and Schwerner's parents had wanted him buried in Mississippi with Chaney. But this proved impossible. There is no way to bury a white man with a Negro in Mississippi—unless you bury them at night in a dam. No white undertaker in Mississippi would bury Schwerner anywhere; and no Negro undertaker will touch a white body. He'd be out of business if he did.

That evening, after Chaney's burial, about two hundred Negroes and a few out-of-state whites staged a "march" through part of Meridian to a Negro Baptist church where they held a memorial service for Chaney. Meridian police gave permission for the march and issued "special permits" for every white person who was in it. The Negroes in the march provoked no violence, but the whites in the march were jeered at and bottles were thrown at them by white Mississippians. White women stood in doorways and shouted: "Nigger-lovers!" and "White girl, you're marching with a nigger now, but you'll soon be in your grave like those others!"

About seven hundred persons, all but a few of them Negroes, were in the church for the memorial service for Chaney. This surprised a Negro preacher. He told me: "I was amazed at the size of the crowd. Fifteen years ago you couldn't have gotten ten people to stick their heads out of the door and associate with such a service."

The principal speaker at Chaney's memorial service was David Dennis, the CORE field secretary in Mississippi and assistant program director for COFO. Here is some of what he said:

> I don't grieve for James Chaney. He lived a fuller life than many of us will ever live. He's got his freedom, and we're still fighting for ours. I'm sick and tired of going to the funerals of black men who have been murdered by white men. . . .
>
> I've got vengeance in my heart tonight, and I ask you to feel angry with me. I'm sick and tired, and I ask you to be sick and tired with me. The white men who murdered James Chaney are never going to be punished. I ask you to be sick and tired of that. I'm tired of the people of this country allowing this thing to continue to happen. . . .
>
> I'm tired of that old suggestion that Negroes ought to go back to Africa. I'm ready to go back to Africa the day when all the Jews, the Poles, the Russians, the Germans and the Anglo-Saxons go back where they came from. This land was taken from the Indians, and it belongs just as much to us Negroes as it does to any other group. . . .
>
> We've got to stand up. The best way we can remember James Chaney is to demand our rights. Don't just look at me and go back and tell folks you've been to a nice service. Your work is just beginning. And I'm going to tell you deep down in my heart what I feel right now. If you go back home and sit down and take what these white men in Mississippi are doing to us . . . if you take it and don't do something about it . . . then God damn your souls!

Stand up! Those neighbors who were too afraid to come to this service, pick them up and take them down there to register to vote! Go down there and do it! Don't ask that white man *if* you can register to vote. Just tell him: "Baby, I'm here!" Stand up! Hold your heads up! Don't bow down anymore! We want our freedom NOW! I don't want to go to another funeral like this. I'm tired of such funerals. . . . [Starts to cry] I'm tired of it! You've got to stand up! [Breaks down and sobs]

Separate memorial services were held in New York for Schwerner and Goodman, after which Goodman was buried in Mount Judah Cemetery, Cypress Hills, Brooklyn. Traditional Jewish graveside services were held. Schwerner's body was cremated.

The New York *Herald Tribune* story on the service for Goodman reported:

The principal eulogy was given by Rabbi Arthur Lelyveld, of Cleveland, a friend of the Goodman family. He was beaten by segregationists in Mississippi last month when he visited the state as a counselor to the young workers in the "Mississippi Project."

Rabbi Lelyveld stressed that the work for which Mr. Goodman and his friends died must go forward. Those who carry it on are a "living and dynamic" memorial to the three young men, he said.

"These are the young men who are patiently instructing the old and the young in their citizenship rights; who are offering fellowship to the dispossessed; and who, as they go from door to door for voter registration or teach in freedom schools, give to the Negro community of Mississippi the assurance they are not alone," he said.

He described Mr. Goodman as a "proud and self-accepting Jew," and said that the "tradition out of which he came always has known that martyrdom is an ever-possible crown to genuine conviction."

The other speakers were Martin Popper, a lawyer and a family friend, and Ralph Engleman and Barbara Jones, classmates of Mr. Goodman at Queens College.

Mr. Popper said that Mr. Goodman and his friends were national heroes. The title "civil-rights worker" has become part of the language of hope, in the way that "abolitionist" and "underground railway" did 100 years ago, he said.

Mr. Black closed the service by reminding the mourners that they had a responsibility in the cause for which Mr. Goodman died. "It's very easy," he said, "to criticize others for the evil that made this day . . . the question today is not whether Andrew Goodman is dead—the question is whether we are dead."

At the end of the service, a man stepped forward and handed the rose on the coffin to Mrs. Goodman. She moved into the center aisle, then turned back and took the arm of Mrs. Chaney. They went out together behind the coffin, followed by Michael Schwerner's mother and his wife, and by Mr. Goodman and Mr. Schwerner's father, who had joined hands.

On August 16, exactly two months after the church was burned, a memorial service was held for the three in the "ashes" of the Mount Zion Methodist Church at Longdale. Negroes sat on wooden benches among the trees. Sheriff Rainey and Deputy Price stood apart and looked on and listened.

Ben Chaney, James' eleven-year-old brother, made a speech. He closed with: "And I want us all to stand up here together and say just one thing. I want the sheriff to hear this good. WE AIN'T SCARED NO MORE OF SHERIFF RAINEY!"

Mrs. Fannie Lee Chaney, James' mother, said: "I said I wasn't going to say nothing, but I can't come up here and not say something. When my child drove nights out here to this church, who grudged him so much that they thought they had to kill him? Mickey Schwerner, he was like a son of mine. James told me: 'Mama, that man's got sense. He's down here to help us. I'm not gonna let him do it by hisself. I'm going with him. I'm gonna stand up by his side.' That was my child, as well as Mickey and Andy. And I just don't want those children's work to be in vain."

Robert Moses, program director of COFO and head of the Mississippi Project, said: "The tragedy here is the work of people who believed in an idea enough to kill for it. The problem of Mississippi is the problem of the nation and of the world. A way has to be found to change this desire to kill."

A Negro preacher from Neshoba County, the Rev. Clinton Collier, said: "All the cops in Neshoba County will not be able to kill this cause. This Heaven which the white man has made for himself in Neshoba County, it's hell for us. Lord, give us strength to make a Heaven for ourselves here, too."

At the conclusion of the service at Longdale they all held hands and sang: "Take My Hand, Precious Lord, Lead Me Home."

. . .

The executive director of the Protestant Council of New York

City, Dr. Dan Potter, proposed that the three be buried in Arlington National Cemetery. He said: "These young men gave their lives in the cause of liberty as truly and heroically as any American ever has in war or peace. They deserve the deepest gratitude and highest honor that all Amerrican can bestow upon them, for they died for the liberty of us all."

. . .

What about "dying in vain?" Did Schwerner, Chaney, and Goodman die in vain, or did their lives and the manner of their deaths contribute something to racial progress in Mississippi and elsewhere? Is the glacier moving? If so, is some of the movement due to a murder which was intended to halt movement?

In January 1965 I put the question to Alvin Fielder, the Negro druggist in Meridian in whose building the Community Center was located.

"Well," Mr. Fielder said, "it depends on how you look at it. In some ways yes, in some ways no."

There is little visible evidence that Mickey and Rita and James Chaney accomplishd anything in Meridian. The variety store in the Negro section still has the one "visible Negro" employee. The other stores appear unchanged. Perhaps there are a few more registered Negro voters. The NAACP in Mississippi has withdrawn from COFO; and the NAACP leaders, like Albert Jones in Meridian who befriended Mickey and Rita, feel that the "bearded beatniks" have outlived their usefulness and that now, with the Civil Rights Act, they should leave. Mickey and Rita had broken with Jones before the murder

Men like Mr. Jones are also concerned about God. "The church is important to Mississippi Negroes," he told me in his home in January 1965. "Even as we become militant and fight for our rights, we still want to retain our religion. Some of the white ones who come in here are not reverent and religious, so they have a limited understanding of our people. I want to fight as much as anybody for Negro advancement. My windows have been shot out and blasted out. I want the ballot for Negroes, better jobs, better education, and I don't want Negroes looked down on any more. But the church is still our mighty fortress, and I want it to stay that way. We can't always be going to jail. Now that we have the right to, we need to walk through the front door at City Hall and sit down and talk with the mayor. He's the one we have to live with, and he's the one I persuaded to hire five Negro policemen before COFO ever came. And I don't see anything

wrong with bathing and shaving and putting on a necktie before I go to City Hall, or to church, or to eat in a restaurant
with either Negroes or white folks."

Perhaps the most important "good" done by Mickey
Schwerner and James Chaney in life, and by all three of
them in death, lies in the hearts of Mississippi Negroes. Most
everybody agrees: "Things will never be the same again." By
this they mean that Negroes will never again be as apathetic
as before the Outsiders came. And whites cannot be as in-
transigent. The march toward a better deal for Negroes has
begun, and it is not likely to stop in Mississippi or elsewhere.

. . .

What of the murderers? What manner of men are they?
What will become of them?

Over the months I observed and studied several of them.
They always reminded me of the six who surrounded Edward
Aaron in the "lair" near Birmingham, and "interrogated"
him, and "took his nuts" to prove that one of them was worthy of promotion. The castrators of Aaron wanted to send
him "out on the street to show Earl Warren and Martin Luther King what we think of them." The murderers of the
three were trying to "get at Earl Warren and Lyndon Johnson and Martin Luther King and everybody who looks down
on Mississippi."

One of the murderers said: "We couldn't get at them
South-haters in Washington. But we could get at them three
we had. So we showed 'em." Every one of the murderers
seems to believe that "we showed" somebody something.

In his book *Mississippi: The Closed Society*, Professor
James W. Silver describes the white-supremacy terrorists in
these words:

> [There is] an anxious, fearful, frustrated group of marginal
> white men, who exist in every Mississippi community. It
> makes no difference whether these people are suffering from
> their own personal inadequacies or whether they are over-
> whelmed by circumstances: they escaped from their troubles
> periodically into the excitement of racial conflict. They are
> impelled to keep the Negro down in order to look up to
> themselves. . . . Racial bigotry transcends reason in Missis-
> sippi because, for varying motives, so many leaders are will-
> ing to exploit the nameless dreads and alarms that have taken
> possession of most white people. The poor whites may not
> raise their low standard of living by blaming it on Negroes,
> but they do release an aggressive energy upon a socially ac-
> cepted scapegoat. Themselves last in everything else, they can

still rejoice in having the "nigger" beneath them. At least in the short run, nearly every white man does stand to derive economic, political, or social status from keeping Negroes in their place.

I have written earlier that the white slayer of a Negro once asked me: "If I ain't better'n a goddam, black-assed nigger, then what the hell am I better'n of?"

What sets the murderers of Schwerner, Chaney, and Goodman apart from the Mafia, from Murder, Incorporated, and from the gangsters of movies and television is that basically they are not ordinary criminal types with police records, they didn't do it for money, and they think they did right. The crimes against humanity which are hardest to understand, and therefore hardest to punish, have always been those committed by "good" men who thought they were doing the Will of God. The Holy Bible is not only present, it's brandished. Murder is done in God's Name. In just about every Klan group is at least one hot-eyed, hard-handed preacher eager to wash his hard hands in the warm, red blood of infidels and "nigger-lovers."

Among the murderers are men who need to believe and to say "niggers ain't smart enough to cause all this trouble. The nigger ain't really to blame. The pore, ignorant nigger, who can't never learn much with his little ape-brain, he's just being used by the Jews and Communists who are causing all the trouble. The Jews and Communists are just a-waitin' till they can use niggers to kill us white men, and let big buck niggers get at our wives and daughters and mongrelize us."

Momentarily, I comforted one of the murderers, then left him confused.

I said: "Well, you were correct on one point. You killed Schwerner because you said he was an 'agitating, trouble-making nigger-loving, Communist, atheistic, Jew outsider.' It's true that he called himself an atheist."

"He did, huh? He didn't believe in *nothing?*"

"Oh, yes," I said, "he believed in something. He believed devoutly."

"What'd he believe in?"

"He believed in *you!*"

"In me! What the hell!"

"Yeah," I said. "He believed in you. He believed love could conquer hate. He believed love could change even you. He didn't think you were hopeless. That's what got him killed."

As I say, that left him somewhat confused.

THE TRIAL*

When the trial finally began, three years and four months after the murder, it sounded as dated as *We Shall Overcome*. The Movement had changed. Mickey Schwerner, Andy Goodman and Jim Chaney had gone out of fashion.

But the opponents had not changed. The United States of America versus White Supremacy. Representing the United States, from Washington, was the same attorney, John Doar, lanky, dogged, phlegmatic, who fought to protect Freedom Riders in 1961. So soft-spoken he sometimes sounds dull, Doar nodded when the twelve defense lawyers began by telling the jury that he was the enemy—the same spokesman for the hated Justice Department who "forced the Negro James Meredith into the University of Mississippi."

Doar had come to try eighteen alleged conspirators. The defense lawyers had come to try "a Jew-atheist mixer" and "Washington."

The defendants, all identified as Ku Klux Klansmen, were in their Sunday suits, with neckties. They were:

SAM HOLLOWAY BOWERS JR., from Laurel, 43, single, dapper, operator of the Magnolia Consolidated Realty Company and the Sambo Amusement Company (vending machines). . . . Identified as the Imperial Wizard of the White Knights of the Ku Klux Klan. . . . Born in New Orleans, five feet 11 inches tall, sandy hair.

ALTON WAYNE ROBERTS, Meridian, 29, mobile homes salesman, played football at Meridian high school. . . . Served in the Marine Corps, 1957-58, and, according to the FBI, received a bad conduct discharge for fighting, drunkenness and absence without leave. . . . Worked a year as a bouncer at the Skyview nightclub. . . . Married, three children; six feet two inches tall, long black hair.

* This entire chapter was written after the trial.

CECIL RAY PRICE, 29, deputy sheriff, Neshoba County, born in Jackson, Miss., and finished high school. Married, one child; six feet tall, 225 pounds.

HORACE DOYLE BARNETTE, 29, automotive parts salesman for Allen Supply Company in Meridian until three days after discovery of the bodies, then went to Cullen, La. . . . . Born in Plain Dealing, La., where he finished high school. . . . Came to Meridian in May, 1964. . . . Married, bald, six feet tall, 180 pounds.

JIMMY ARLEDGE, 30, Meridian truck driver. . . . Born in Newton County, Miss., completed tenth grade in high school. . . . Married, six feet tall, 145 pounds.

BILLY WAYNE POSEY, 30, manager of Phillips 66 Service Station in Williamsville, near Philadelphia, Miss. . . . Born in Neshoba County, married, four children; six feet two inches tall.

JIMMY SNOWDEN, 34, truck driver for Meridian laundry. . . . Born in Bailey, Miss, and attended Meridian Junior College two years. . . . In Army 1954-56, discharged a corporal. . . . Married, three children; five feet 10 inches tall, 140 pounds.

Bowers was not placed at the murder scene. But, according to testimony, the other six men named above—Roberts, Price, Doyle, Barnette, Arledge, Posey and Snowden—were six of the seven men who were present at the scene on Rock Cut road, when the three were murdered. One of these six men, according to testimony, shot and killed both Schwerner and Goodman. The seventh man at the scene, according to testimony, was:

JAMES E. JORDAN, 41, construction worker, Meridian, who gave information to the FBI in 1964 and thereafter lived in Georgia and elsewhere under FBI protection. According to testimony, but not according to his own confession, he killed James Chaney with three shots from a revolver. Jordan was the nineteenth man indicted for conspiracy, but, since he was a government witness he was not tried with the other eighteen.

The other eleven defendants were Lawrence Rainey, 43, sheriff of Neshoba County; E. G. (Hop) Barnette, 47, sheriff-elect of Neshoba County; Rev. Edgar Ray Killen, Baptist preacher, 42, Neshoba County; Olen Burrage, 42, farmer and truck operator, Neshoba County; Herman Tucker, 40, bulldozer operator, Neshoba County; Jerry Sharpe, 27, Pulpwood buyer, Neshoba County; Richard A. Willis, 65, city policeman, Philadelphia, Miss.; Travis Barnette, 34, Meridian mechanic; Bernard L. Akin, 45, Meridian, dealer in mobile

homes; Frank Herndon, Meridian, cafe operator, 44; and
James Harris, 32, Meridian truck driver.

The bodies were found on property owned by Burrage. According to testimony, the bodies were covered by a bulldozer
owned by Tucker. According to testimony, the Meridian
group first began gathering at a cafe owned by Herndon, then
moved to the mobile homes court owned by Akin.

Presiding over the court was U. S. District Judge William
Harold Cox, 66, a lifelong associate of U. S. Senator James
Eastland. They both were born in Sunflower County; they
roomed together at the University of Mississippi; then they
were law partners.

Again: the eighteen defendants were being tried, not for
murder, since murder is not a federal offense, but for "conspiring to violate the civil rights" of the victims. The maximum penalty was ten years and a fine of $5000.

Change was evident in the assembled group of prospective
jurors. For three years Judge Cox had worked to make the
jury list in his district conform to Supreme Court decisions
requiring that jury lists must be representative of the population as to race, sex, and educational achievement. About half
the prospective jurors were women, about a third were
Negroes, many of them with high school or college educations.

The method by which the jurors were selected favored the
defendants. Judge Cox qualified, then presented fifty men and
women to opposing counsel. Thirty-one whites, nineteen
Negroes. Thirty-eight were to be struck; the remaining twelve
were to be the jury. By law each side has ten strikes. But since
the eighteen defendants were being tried together, the judge
allowed the twelve defense attorneys an additional strike for
each defendant. This meant that of the fifty prospective jurors, twenty-eight would be struck by the defense, ten by the
government.

The defense used nineteen of its strikes to remove the
Negroes. The government used its ten strikes to remove the
white men and women who seemed most likely to favor or
fear the Klan. Then, armed with a report on each prospective
juror's racial attitudes and economic position, the defense
struck the nine white men and women who seemed most
likely to feel able to defy the Klan.

Here are the remaining twelve, the jury, seven women and
five men:

LANGSTON SMITH ANDERSON, 45, of Lumberton, an
engineer engaged in oil exploration and a member of the
Mississippi Agricultural and Industrial Board. (Which seeks

new industry for the state.) Judge Cox appointed him foreman of the jury.

MRS. S. M. GREEN, 67, of Route 5, Hattiesburg, housewife.

MRS. LESSIE LOWREY, 52, of Wayne County, grocery store owner.

HOWARD ORREN WINBORN, 56, Petal, pipe fitter.

HARMON WILLIAM RASBERRY, 32, Stonewall, textile worker.

GUSSIE BAUCUM STATON, 64, Union, housewife.

JESSIE PAUL HOLLINGSWORTH, 48, Moss Point, electrician.

MRS. JAMES C. HEFLIN, 36, Lake, industrial worker.

NELL BOND DEDEAUX, Lumberton, housewife.

WILLIE V. ARNESEN, 58, Meridian, secretary.

EDSELL Z. PARKS, 34, Brandon, station clerk.

ADELAIDE H. COMER, 43, Ocean Springs, cafeteria cook.

One of the early government witnesses was Rev. Charles Johnson, of Meridian, a Negro preacher and employee of the Poverty Program. He said he knew Mickey Schwerner during his stay in Meridian and attended meetings with him in Lauderdale County. "He was interested in some of the things I was interested in," the witness said. "Voter registration, upgrading jobs, better pay, and police treatment of Negroes. He went to these different towns and communities to organize voter registrations."

Reverend Johnson was cross-examined by Laurel Weir, a defense lawyer.

"Did you hear Schwerner advocate that we should not be fighting in Vietnam?"

"No, sir."

"Did you hear him advocate the burning of draft cards?"

"No, sir."

"Well, Schwerner was an atheist. Did you ever offer to pray with him?"

"We had prayer at meetings," Johnson answered.

"Did he pray?"

"I wasn't looking. I was praying."

Then Weir asked this question: "Isn't it true that you and Mr. Schwerner undertook to get young male Negroes to sign a statement that they would rape a white woman every week in the hot summer of 1964?"

"Did we do what?" Johnson asked.

Weir repeated the question, slowly, emphatically. Judge

Cox snapped: "I hope you know that this line of questioning is highly improper!"

Weir said the question had been handed to him on a piece of paper.

"Then who wrote that question?" Judge Cox demanded. "I want to know which attorney wrote such a question."

After a pause, Rev. Edgar Ray Killen raised his hand. Judge Cox said: "I'm not going to allow this trial to be made into a farce! Imagine a question like that! And coming from a preacher, too! I'm talking about you, Killen!"

When the government began bringing up the paid informers, the defense lawyers began yelling "Judas!" and the "thirty pieces of silver." The 27-year-old Meridian Methodist minister, Delmar Dennis, made a convincing witness. Well-educated, he had been a member of the Lauderdale County Klavern, White Knights of the Ku Klux Klan, almost since it was organized in February, 1964. He is a Mason, a Shriner, a Knight Templar, and an active member of the Lauderdale County chapter of the John Birch Society. He says he is a segregationist, and a "strong conservative." "But I don't believe violence is the answer," he said.

Bowers had appointed Dennis a Klan Titan (district leader), and while he was serving the Klan, in close association with Bowers, Dennis was being paid about $5000 a year by the FBI and was making almost daily reports on Klan activities.

It was Dennis who connected Bowers with the conspiracy, and who told of seeing most of the other defendants at Klan meetings. Dennis had been at the meeting in Neshoba County on June 16th; and he told of a conversation with Price about the murder three months after it had been committed.

Jordan's performance was melodramatic and dull. The defendants had known for three years that Jordan was "in the hands of the FBI." Two days before he testified, six FBI agents, with guns drawn, ushered him into the building where the trial was in progress, and he promptly fainted. They rushed him to a hospital with a reported heart attack. But two days later they brought him back, and he took the stand. Pale, drawn, almost completely bald, he testified in a monotone and never looked at the defendants.

He told of Killen's coming to Meridian; of the meeting first at Herndon's cafe, then at Akin's mobile home court; of the two carloads of men who then went to Philadelphia. He named everybody. He told of the chase, and how the motorcade approached the murder spot. Then he sprang his surprise. He said he got out of a car, served as a lookout, and was four hundred yards away from the party when he heard "shots and doors slamming." He said he then walked to the murder spot, saw the three bodies lying in the road, helped load them into a car, and went to the burial site.

In short, Jordan confessed to *conspiracy* but not to murder. He insisted he didn't witness a murder and didn't know who fired the shots. But he did know the names of most of the men at the murder scene.

(Had Jordan confessed to killing one of the three, he would have risked being arrested by Sheriff Rainey and Deputy Price, and being tried for murder in Neshoba County.)

Then the government and Judge Cox performed a maneuver which may be without precedent. On November 20, 1964, in a motel in Louisiana, Horace Doyle Barnette signed a statement for two FBI agents. It was a full confession, naming everyone Barnette knew. Subsequently, Barnette repudiated this confession, pleaded not guilty to the indictment, and stood trial with the other defendants, including his brother, Travis Barnette. The government moved to have this confession read into the record.

Judge Cox studied the statement, then ruled that since Horace Doyle Barnette was a defendant, his statement could not be used against his fellow defendants. The judge further ruled that the Barnette statement could be used against Jordan, since Jordan was not a defendant but a government witness. The judge then deleted all names from the statement except Jordan's. He made some further deletions, after which he allowed an FBI agent to read this strange "blank-blank-blank" statement to the jury and into the record.

Here is the statement from the record. To make it easier to read and to discuss I have substituted words like Somebody and Somewhere for the blanks.

Springhill, La.
November 20, 1964

I do hereby make this free and voluntary statement to SA (Special Agent) Henry Rask and SA James A. Wooten, who have identified themselves to me to be special agents of the Federal Bureau of Investigation, and SA Henry Rask has informed me that I do not have to make a statement, that any statement made by me can be used against me in a court of law, and that I am entitled to consult with an attorney before making this statement, and that if I cannot afford an attorney and I am required to appear in court, the court will appoint one for me. No force, threats or promises were made to induce me to make this statement.

I presently reside at Cullen, La. I am 26 years old and was born on September 11, 1938, at Plaindealing, La.

On June 21, 1964, about 8 P.M., I was having supper at Somebody's house, Meridian, Miss. Somebody called Somebody on the telephone and told Somebody that the Klan had a job and wanted to know if Somebody and I would go. Somebody asked me if I would go and we went to Somewhere in Meridian, Miss. We did not know what the job was.

Upon arriving at Somewhere we were met by Somebody, Somebody, Jim Jordan and Somebody.

Somebody told us that three civil rights workers were in jail in Philadelphia, Miss., and that they were going to be released from jail and that we were going to catch them and give them a whipping. We were given brown cloth gloves (several words deleted here).

Somebody, Somebody and Jordan got into my car and we drove to Philadelphia. Somebody and Somebody left before we did and we were told that we would meet them there. (More words deleted)

When we arrived in Philadelphia about 9:30 P.M., we met Somebody (deletion) and wait for someone to tell us when the three civil rights workers were being released from jail.

While we were talking, Somebody stated that "we have a place to bury them and a man to run the Something to cover them up." That was the first time I realized that the three civil rights workers were to be killed.

About five or ten minutes after we parked, Somebody came to the car and said "they are going toward Meridian on Highway 19." We proceeded out Highway 19 and caught up to a Mississippi State Patrol car, which pulled into a store on the left hand side of the road. We pulled alongside the Patrol car and then another car from somewhere pulled in between us. I was driving a 1957 Ford, four door, two-tone blue, bearing Louisiana licenses.

(Major deletions here)

Somebody then drove away and we followed. (Deletion) I then drove fast and caught up to the car that the three civil rights workers were in, pulled over to the side of the road and stopped. About a minute or two later, Somebody came along and stopped on the pavement beside my car. Jordan asked him who was going to stop them and Somebody said he would (deletion) and we followed. The civil rights workers turned off Highway 19 on to a side road and drove about a couple of miles before (major deletion).

Somebody told them to get out and get into his car. (Major deletion) At the junction of Highway 19 and where we turned off, I had let Somebody out of the car to signal the fellows in the (blank) car. We then turned around and proceeded back toward Philadelphia. The first car to start back was Somebody and he had Jim Jordan in the front seat with him and the three civil rights workers in the back seat. I followed next and picked up Somebody at the Junction of Highway 19. Somebody drove the 1963 Ford belonging to the civil rights workers.

When we came to Somebody's car, Somebody and Somebody pulled over to the left side of the highway and stopped in front of Somebody's car. I stopped behind it. Somebody and Somebody and the other men from Somewhere got into the 1963 Ford and rode with Somebody. I do not know how many men were from somewhere. Somebody then started first and I pulled in behind him and Somebody driving the 1963 Ford came last.

I followed Somebody down Highway 19 and he turned left on to the gravel road. About a mile up the road he stopped and Somebody and I stopped behind him, with about a car length between each car. Before I could get out of the car Somebody ran past my car to Somebody's car, opened the left rear door, pulled Schwerner out of the car, spun him around so that Schwerener was standing on the left side of the road, with his back to the ditch, and said "Are you that nigger lover?" and Schwerner said, "Sir, I know just how you feel." Somebody had a pistol in his right hand, then shot Schwerner. Somebody then went back to Somebody's car and got Goodman, took him to the left side of the road with Goodman facing the road, and shot Goodman.

When Somebody shot Schwerner, Somebody had his hand on Schwerner's shoulder. When Somebody shot Goodman, Somebody was standing within reach of him.

Schwerner fell to the left so that he was lying alongside the road. Goodman spun around and fell back toward the bank in back.

At this time, Jim Jordan said "save one for me." He then got out of Somebody's car and got Chaney out. I remember Chaney backing up, facing the road, and standing on the bank on the other side of the ditch and Jordan stood in the middle of the road and shot him. I do not remember how many times Jordan shot. Jordan then said "You didn't leave me anything but a nigger, but at least I killed me a nigger."

The three civil rights workers were then put in the back of their 1963 Ford wagon. I do not know who put the bodies in the car, but I only put Chaney's foot inside the car.

Somebody then got into his car and drove back toward Highway 19. Somebody, Somebody and Jordan then got into the 1963 Ford and started up the road. Somebody, Somebody and another person who I do not know the name of got into my car and we followed. I do not know the roads we took, but we went through the outskirts of Philadelphia and to the dam site (deletion).

When we arrived at the dam site, someone said that the Something operator was not there and Somebody and Somebody and I went in my car to find him. We drove out to a paved road and about a mile down the road we saw a Something parked on the left side of the road. Somebody told me to stop and we backed up to this car. Somebody said that they were already down there and Somebody said to follow them. I followed the Something back toward the dam site, taking a different road, until the Something stopped. Somebody said "It's just a little ways over there," and Somebody and the Something operator walked the rest of the way. (Major deletion)

Somebody and I then followed Somebody and the other man back to Somewhere. (Major deletion)

We were there about thirty minutes when the other fellows came from the dam site in the 1963 Ford. Somebody got a glass gallon jug and filled it with gasoline to be used to burn the 1963 Ford owned by the three civil rights workers. (Deletion) It was then about 1 or 1:30 in the morning.

Somebody, Somebody, Jordan, Somebody and I then got into my car and we drove back toward Philadelphia. When we got to Philadelphia a Something stopped us and we got out. Somebody, Somebody, Somebody and Somebody who told us which way the civil rights workers were leaving town, got out of the Something. This was about 2 A.M., June 22, 1964. (Deletion) We talked for two or three minutes and then someone said that we better not talk about this and Somebody said "I'll kill anyone who talks, even if it was my own brother."

We then got back into my car and drove back to Meridian and passed Somebody's car which was still parked alongside the road. We then kept going to Meridian. I took Somebody home, left Jordan and Somebody Someplace, took Somebody home and went home myself.

I have read the above statement, consisting of this and nine other pages and they are true and correct to the best of my knowledge and belief. I have signed my initials to the bottom of the first nine pages and initialed mistakes. No force, threats or promises were made to induce me to make this statement.

Horace Doyle Barnette
(Signature)

Witnessed:

Henry Rask, Special Agent, FBI, Nov. 20, 1964

James A. Wooten, Special Agent, FBI, New Orleans, La. 11-20-64.

So five months after the murder, and three years before
the trial, the FBI knew who all the Somebodies were. They
knew what official cars were Where and did What, and Who
threatened Whom if Anybody talked. The State of Mississippi
knew all this, too: at least the governor and the attorney-gen-
eral did. I knew much of it. The problem was to bring somebody to trial and make it all publishable.

Even in 1967, at a conspiracy trial, the United States of
America had to use Jordan to identify some of the Somebodies, then use Barnette's emasculated statement against Jordan.
And from none of the government witnesses could the defense lawyers find out and make public who told the FBI,
on August 2, 1964, where the bodies were.

The defendants did not testify. They listened while a hundred witnesses testified to their good character, their peaceful
reputations, their "service in the cause of Christ Jesus." Several Baptist preachers testified to the "Godliness" of Reverend Edgar Ray Killen, to "his fervent ministry for the Lord
Jesus Christ" . . . "his moving funerals and wedding ceremo-
nies." A Baptist deacon insisted that the Imperial Wizard,
Sam Bowers, was "a devoted Baptist, a man who has had an
experience with the Lord."

I watched the jurors. Judge Cox allowed them to keep note-
books, and I noticed how often and how much some of the
women wrote in them. I watched them while the defense lawyers, summing up, waved the confederate flag and damned the
meddlers, the mixers, and the mongrelizers. I watched them
while John Doar, in his flat, Midwestern voice, said quietly:
"For you, ladies and gentlemen, to find these defendants not
guilty would be to deny that there was a nighttime release
from jail, to deny that there was a nighttime recapture using
the emblems of authority, to deny that there was a nighttime
murder, to deny that there was a nighttime burial with a bulldozer in an earthen dam. For yourselves, for Mississippi, for
America, for all humanity, you must find the courage to confront these guilty men and order them punished."

Then I left Mississippi—completely convinced that the jury
would never bring a guilty verdict. By telephone, to New
York and elsewhere, I told my friends and associates that a
guilty verdict was impossible. "Those are little people," I explained. "Some of them are quite poor. Some of them live
out on the edges of small communities, far back in the piney
woods. How can they afford to take the risks?"

When the jury had been out three days; when they had repeatedly reported to the judge that they were in hopeless dis-

agreement; and when, each time, he had sent them back; I called a knowledgeable lawyer in Meridian and asked him if he thought a guilty verdict was possible.

"Not a chance in the world," he said. Those people would have to be crazy to defy the Klan on this case."

But we were wrong. Next day the jury brought in a verdict. It was, obviously, a compromise verdict. But it was a verdict. The jurors found guilty six of the seven men they thought were at the murder site. Roberts, Price, Doyle Barnette, Arledge, Posey and Snowden. To these six, they added Bowers. He was so startled by the verdict that he froze, paled, then bolted and ran from photographers.

On Killen, Hop Barnette, and Sharpe the jurors declared they could not agree on a verdict. They found the other eight not guilty.

The "moderate" newspapers in Mississippi shouted with joy. "Magnificent!" said the *Delta Democrat-Times* of Greenville. The Tupelo *Journal* called it "a turning point in race relations." The Vicksburg *Post* expressed "profound satisfaction" and added: "This jury was composed of Mississippi citizens who have proved that Mississippians can be as conscientious as the people of any other state." The most disgruntled daily in the state, the Jackson *Clarion-Ledger,* waited three days, then congratulated the jury, the judge, and Mississippi on the verdict.

In December, 1967, Judge Cox passed sentence on the seven. He sentenced Bowers and Roberts to ten years, Price to six years, and the others to four years in federal prison. The story will continue, but at this point the immediate fate of these seven is before the Fifth Circuit Court of Appeals.

Afterword

William Bradford Huie's writings on the civil rights movement stand as a singular achievement. That is not necessarily good. There is no historical overview in his work. There is no recounting of political dynamics. And there is none of the historian's or journalist's standard attempt at impartiality by writing about dynamic events in an omniscient, third-person voice.

Instead, Huie gives the reader a first-person, in-your-face, argumentative presence in every story. His dealings with segregationists, killers and civil rights workers, and his own sense of events as a white southern man is all at the heart of Huie's unique contribution to the history of the Civil Rights Movement.

I discovered Huie's work on the movement while writing *Eyes on the Prize–America's Civil Rights Years 1954–1965*. My research into the 1955 murder of Emmett Till had taken me to interviews, government archives, books, and newspaper stories. A few sources made reference to Huie's writings but noted the he had paid the alleged killers for interviews. Some identified Huie as a novelist or fiction writer who was dabbling in the all too real horror of a murder. The descriptions of Huie created deep doubts about the credibility of his work.

But once I picked up Huie's work all the other documents and interviews faded to pale, bloodless sketches of the story. Here was a vivid, violent, alive report. Here was a detailed telling full of human stupidity, sexual fear, racism, turns of fate, and cruel death. There was no attempt by the writer to disguise his voice or his role in events. In fact, Huie's urgent voice was central to the telling of the murder of Till, a teenaged black boy who had whistled at a white woman. The writer's emotional narrative of a real story bordered on the best American fiction. He had created a riveting non-fiction story using fictional techniques on par with Truman Capote's work for *In Cold Blood*, or Norman Mailer's techniques in *Executioner's Song*.

In the Till story, Huie took his readers inside the minds of grown white men beating a teenaged black boy, then stripping him naked, tying a large cotton gin fan to his leg, and then shooting him in the head. The savagery of the act, the fear of sexual flirtation between black boys and white girls and the boy's inability to sense his approaching death, all came to life in Huie's writing. For historians of the civil rights movement Huie's account stands as the crowning jewel of all writing on that sad case. Research has to be done by anyone seeking to understand the larger context. But once the research is done and the background is in place any reader wanting to see and feel the central act in detail has to go to Huie. His rendering of the key event–the murder–stands out for two reasons: It is brilliantly written and it is available no where else.

At the start of this book, *Three Lives for Mississippi*, Huie gives similarly vivid treatment to the KKK's castration of a black man. News accounts and hospital records can tell you about the who, what, where, and when of the cruel act. But it is Huie alone who gives readers and historians the inside account from the people doing the cutting and the man who was cut. When Huie has the villainous racists speeding back to recover a forgotten cup filled with the man's detached testicles, the human farce is in full force and the reader realizes that this is too absurd to be anything but the sad, ringing truth.

In *Three Lives for Mississippi*, Huie's singular skills are required to explain a triple-murder that standard journalistic techniques did not penetrate. Here is an act cloaked from public view and rational comprehension by cultural resentments as well as racial hatreds and small town loyalties. At first, Huie appears as the writer who knows what is going on from the moment he is told that the three civil rights workers are missing. Even so, he doesn't want to take on the job of peeling back the layers of deceit to reveal the "why," and the "how," of the horror. He was still stung by the reaction to his writings on the Till murder.

In the Till case, nearly ten years earlier, Huie's payment of thousands of dollars to the murderers was harshly criticized as unethical journalism that cast suspicion on him for rewarding murderers with money. Suspicion also fell on the information provided by the killers because it might have been concocted simply to get the money that was being offered. But later historical work on the case supported the quality and truth of Huie's account. His long-standing defense of his reporting techniques–that he wanted the truth and was willing to get at it in any way, including paying for it–suddenly had a track record to back it up. That is why editors began calling him in June 1964 once it was evident that the civil rights workers, James Chaney, Andy Goodman, and Mickey Schwerner, were missing and probably dead.

Huie did not disappoint the editors or his readers. In *Three Lives for Mississippi*, he once again combines a willingness to pay for information with the intuitions of a native white southerner in mid-century. But given the criticism that followed his telling of the Till murder, Huie was self-conscious about what he was doing. In this edition of the book that self- consciousness is evident as Huie uses italicized paragraphs to annotate the original text. In those paragraphs he matches his account of events, written before the trial of the killers, against the details that became public in later sworn testimony. Huie's reporting was not perfect but it was not far from it. It stood that acid test and his sense of relief is evident in the fact that he points the small areas of difference between his account and what investigators and witnesses later told judge and jury.

And now, over thirty years later, it is also true that Huie's work on the Chaney, Goodman, and Schwerner murders has stood the test of time. Researchers and historians have not contradicted the fine, textured telling of the specifics of the murder act or the motivations of the murderers, as told by Huie. To the contrary, Huie's writing on the case now stands as the best account of the crazed killing of three young activists. His work is key to the 1988 book, *We Are Not Afraid,—The Story of Goodman, Schwerner, and Chaney and the Civil Rights Campaign for Mississippi*, by Seth Cagin and Philip Dray. In that thorough study of the case, Cagin and Dray argue with one point of Huie's speculation [about why the burned car was left for the FBI to find] but never with Huie's version of the facts of how the crime was committed. And they use Huie's detailed account of the murder and Huie's interviews to give their readers a fuller feel for the story.

Huie's work stands as a singular achievement and an important contribution to the civil rights story and to American history. Huie might have settled for the simple praise of having it said that his work is good reading. It is.

Juan Williams

About the Author

From the end of World War II until the middle nineteen-fifties, William Bradford Huie, an Alabama native, was enjoying huge success in the media capitals of the world, New York City and Washington, D.C. Huie had purchased in 1950, from Lawrence Spivak, the old H. L. Mencken magazine *The American Mercury* and was the magazine's editor. (William F. Buckley, Jr., was one of his staff.) In the *Mercury*, Huie was having his say in article after article on matters of national defense, politics, the issues of the day.

He was also, from 1950–1953, co-host/interviewer on the public affairs television program *The Longines Chronoscope*, sponsored by Longines-Wittnauer watches. On this program, a forerunner of *Meet the Press, Face the Nation,* and so on, Huie interviewed such figures as John Foster Dulles, Earl Warren, then-governor of California, Harold Stassen, U.S. Senator Richard Russell of Georgia, and a young member of the U.S. House of Representatives from Massachusetts, John F. Kennedy. Already the author of six books, Huie's exposure on television and in many national magazines, including his own, made him a much sought-after performer on the lecture circuit, and he traveled the United States, speaking about thirty times a year.

Huie was in many ways a man at the height of his powers and at the height of his celebrity, yet in 1957 he moved permanently back to his hometown, Hartselle, Alabama, building a new house for his mother and father and then one for himself and his wife, Ruth, right across the street.

This would seem to be an odd career move for a person in Huie's position, and perhaps not entirely a wise one, but it did put him on the ground at the outset of the movement for civil rights: the right man at the right place at the right time. Huie's return to the South can be explained, and in so doing, one comes to understand a good deal about the man, William Bradford Huie.

Huie was a ninth-generation Southerner. His ancestors lay buried in the cemeteries of northwest Georgia and, for the last three generations, in North Alabama. Born November 13, 1910, to John Bradford Huie and Margaret Lois (Brindley) Huie, William Bradford Huie had graduated valedictorian from his

Hartselle, Alabama high school and became the first in his family to attend college. He had intended to become a professional man, perhaps a doctor or a lawyer, but while still an undergraduate he sold a racy story to *True Story Magazine*, a McFadden Publication, and Huie became determined to become a professional writer. He finished his bachelor's degree in two and one-half years and graduated in January 1930, a member of Phi Beta Kappa. He immediately began what was to become a six-decade-long career of writing, editing, and lecturing, and in that time he was never far from the main action, nearly always in the center of some controversy.

After graduation, Huie went to work as a reporter for the *Birmingham Post* for $14.50 per week. During these early years of the Depression Huie covered stories that would shape his thinking and his methods for the rest of his life. Writing of the labor violence in Birmingham, Huie wrote of greedy, dictatorial bankers and power company executives, of mine and mill owners who hired private armies of Pinkertons to keep the labor unions out and keep the workers cowed. Huie also learned, however, of the methods used by the unions to recruit members. Reluctant workers might be beaten, their homes dynamited, or they might even be shot in their own front yards. Huie covered the coming of the New Deal to Alabama and especially the Tennessee Valley Authority which would unfortunately have to flood huge stretches of his beloved North Alabama in order to tame the Tennessee River, stop the floods that had plagued this region, and bring the electric power that would move the Valley into the modern era. There were two sides to every story, and Huie the journalist was learning to do the digging, interviewing, and research to uncover both sides and then training himself to tell the story objectively, letting praise and blame fall where they would. The important thing was *to get the story*.

Huie's apprenticeship continued through most of the thirties in Alabama. While with the *Post*, 1931–1936, Huie covered the statehouse and legislature in Montgomery, complete with the corruption therein, the trial of the Scottsboro boys, and executions in the state penitentiary. In the Scottsboro case, Huie was, characteristically, independent. He felt that the Scottsboro boys were guilty. The women were ignorant, itinerant, perhaps even of dubious morality, but they were still unwilling victims of rape. In addition, Huie was disgusted with what he considered left-wing propaganda. The Scottsboro boys were not being starved, or tortured, or kept in rat-infested dungeons. In Huie's opinion, they probably received justice.

Roosevelt Wilson, however, was executed for a crime he never committed. Wilson, an African-American, apparently exchanged a ring for sexual favors with a white woman. She subsequently accused him of rape, and Wilson went to the electric chair because he was black, because he had broken the strongest taboo in racist America, and despite the fact that no one believed him guilty of rape.

In 1936 Huie left the *Birmingham Post* and founded, with Robert Baughn, *Alabama Magazine*, which he edited for one year. Dissatisfied with this effort, Huie, along with his brother, Jack, founded the Cullman, Alabama, *Banner* in 1937. In each case Huie, restless, gave away or sold his share of the publication and moved on. From 1938 to 1940 Huie freelanced, traveling the country, including a stay of several months in California. His stories appeared in *Collier's, The Saturday Evening Post, Liberty, Look, everywhere*. Over his career Huie claimed he held the single-issue record sales for three national magazines: *Look, Collier's*, and *Redbook*.

He also wrote his first novel, *Mud on the Stars* (1942). *Mud* is a highly auto-biographical story, with the hero, Peter Garth Lafavor, leaving his Tennessee Valley home to attend the University of Alabama and become a newspaper reporter in Birmingham, in the process undergoing a thorough political and ideological transformation. Lafavor begins as a ferociously self-reliant conservative and slowly comes to understand the need for the New Deal, the TVA, and finally America's entrance into World War II. The novel ends with Lafavor going off to war. He has come to realize that sometimes the individual must adjust to the great historical mass movements of his time.

Mud on the Stars was a bestseller and brought Huie about $160,000 in royalties. In the 1980s Huie would wryly remind audiences that that was a fortune in those days and that he had thought he was a millionaire and would never be broke again; he was set for life, independently wealthy. This proved not to be the case, of course, although the book, like six other Huie books, was made into a Hollywood feature film—*Wild River*, starring Montgomery Clift and Lee Remick and directed by Elia Kazan—and Huie would, over a lifetime of writing, earn and spend several fortunes. He estimated that his total sales topped twenty-eight million dollars.

In the same year as *Mud on the Stars*, Huie also published *The Fight for Air Power*, with the same publisher, L. B. Fischer, the first of what would be many controversial Huie books. The argument of *The Fight for Air Power* is, not surprisingly, that the Army and the Navy have used their influence in Congress to keep their own appropriations high and thus left little for the fledgling Army Air Corps. The response from Army and Navy was predictable and violent.

In spite of the arguments made in *The Fight for Air Power*, in 1943, Huie, married since 1934 to his childhood hometown sweetheart, Ruth Puckett, but childless, went into the United States Navy. Because of his wide experience as a professional writer, Huie was quickly commissioned and went to work as a Public Information Officer for Vice Admiral Ben Moreell, Chief of Civil Engineers and Chief of the Bureau of Yards and Docks. Admiral Moreell was the youngest Vice Admiral in the U.S. Navy and the head of the newly organized Seabees. Huie's job was to familiarize himself with the men and methods of the Construction Battalions and then publicize their work to the world. He did this to perfection in long articles in *The Saturday Evening Post* and *Life* magazine and in his first book on the Seabees, *Can Do! The Story of the Seabees* (1944). Here Huie explains how the Seabees were organized at the outbreak of war in the Pacific and how the older, more mature men of the building trades— plumbers, carpenters, and electricians—went ashore on island after island with the nineteen-year-old Marines, fighting the Japanese and building roads and runways under enemy fire.

Huie island-hopped throughout 1943 and 1944 in the Pacific and then was transferred to England where he then went ashore on D-Day, June 6. His unit was to film the landing, for a documentary entitled *The Navy at Normandy*, but he recounted later how his boat, men, and photographic equipment were swamped and he spent the first several hours of the invasion crouched behind beach obstructions avoiding enemy fire.

After D-Day, it was pretty clear that the Seabees would not be needed in Europe much longer and Huie was granted a discharge from active duty. He then became a civilian war correspondent and returned to the Pacific to cover the Seabees as the war progressed westward toward Okinawa. Huie published his second Seabee book as a civilian, *From Omaha to Okinawa: The Story of the Seabees* (1945).

During the Second World War, although only on active duty for two years, Huie had served in every theater of operations except the Russian front. His experience in this Great Crusade proved to be a massively rich source of material for him. He continued to write nonfiction books, which would soon include another anti-Navy book, *The Case Against the Admirals* (1956). Another book, *The Execution of Private Slovik* (1954), concerning the execution, under orders from Gen. Dwight D. Eisenhower, of the only soldier ever executed for desertion in the American military in the twentieth century, established him as the foremost investigative reporter of his day. *The Hero of Iwo Jima and Other Stories* (1960) sympathetically tells the story of the Pima Indian Ira Hayes who had become famous for his part in the flag-raising on Mount Suribachi and then succumbed to alcoholism under the stress of unwanted celebrity. In the controversial *Hiroshima Pilot* (1964), Huie disclosed publicly that Major Claude Eatherly, who claimed to have led the raid on Hiroshima and dropped the first atom bomb, later to become a hero to the ban-the-bomb movement in America when he repented, had not been there at all. Eatherly had been in a different plane, checking the weather over Hiroshima, and then radioing that weather report to the *Enola Gay*. Huie unearthed the truth; as painful as it was for Eatherly and the many others who had lionized him, Huie was in the truth business.

Besides a shelf of nonfiction, Huie made use of his military experiences in a series of novels. While in Honolulu he had read the book *Honolulu Harlot* by Jean O'Hara. Inspired by her story, Huie wrote *The Revolt of Mamie Stover* (1951), the story of a wartime prostitute who became wealthy by organizing the brothel along the lines of an automobile assembly line. *The Americanization of Emily* (1959) is set in England and on Omaha Beach at D-Day. *Hotel Mamie Stover* (1963) has as its premise free love between consenting adults at a Hawaii resort island.

Hollywood loved Huie's work. *The Hero of Iwo Jima* was made as *The Outsider* starring Tony Curtis. Jane Russell played Mamie in *Mamie in Revolt*, and Julie Andrews and James Garner played in *The Americanization of Emily* (with screenplay by Paddy Chayefsky). Huie was becoming a respected writer on the subject of the military and the Second World War, but it was not to be his only or even necessarily his major subject. The questions of race and civil rights were to figure just as large in his work.

While working at the *American Mercury* in the early 1940s Huie had become acquainted with the black fiction writer and essayist/anthropologist Zora Neale Hurston. Hurston had submitted several pieces to the *Mercury* with Huie as her editor. In January of 1954 Hurston called Huie at his parents' home in Garden City, Alabama, to ask for his help. A black woman in Live Oak, Florida, had been arrested for killing a local physician and the woman, Ruby McCollum, was being held incommunicado, being denied her constitutional rights. Hurston, working for the black newspaper the *Pittsburgh Courier*, was not allowed to see her. Hurston hoped that Huie, a fairly famous white writer, would be allowed in. He was not, and the resulting controversy resulted in Huie's being arrested and jailed for contempt of court. Finally, in 1956, Huie published the book *The Crime of Ruby McCollum*, the first of what would be a series of five books on civil rights, the KKK, violence, and the Second Great Crusade, the crusade for racial justice in the South.

In the early morning hours of Saturday, August 27, 1955, fourteen-year-old Emmett Till, a black boy from Chicago visiting in Mississippi, was murdered in Money, Mississippi. Two days before, he had whistled at or spoken rudely to a white store clerk, Carolyn Bryant, or in some way broken a piece of the byzantine code that governed race relations in Mississippi in the early 1950s. Till had been seized on Friday night by at least two white men, beaten, and finally shot in the head. His body had been tied to a seventy-four-pound cotton gin fan and thrown into the Tallahatchie River where it was found by a fisherman three days later. The murderers, J. W. Milam and Roy Bryant, were arrested for the crime but acquitted after sixty-seven minutes by a jury of twelve local white men in Sumner, county seat of Tallahatchie County. Huie, working at first for *Look* magazine, drove to Money, Mississippi, and there paid Milam and Bryant for their "stories." They were immune from further prosecution under the double jeopardy clause of the U.S. Constitution and, besides, could not resist the cash Huie paid them, two thousand each. For four nights they told their story. Each day he checked those facts. In the investigation of the Till case, Huie not only got the facts, the true story of how and why Till was slain, he seems to have inadvertently invented "checkbook journalism," in which a reporter pays participants in some event, in this case a murder, for their narratives. The Till case is regarded by many, including David Halberstam in his book *The Fifties* (1993), as the start of the modern Civil Rights movement. The cruelty and stupidity of the murder itself, the obvious failure of the criminal justice system, the horror of the onlookers at Till's funeral in Chicago, where Till's mother had the coffin lid opened so that the world could see "what they did to my boy," all these factors, fueled by Huie's revelations—the truth about what really happened, from the mouths of the racist killers themselves—created the outrage that would fuel the Movement, North and South.

The Till case also set up William Bradford Huie as *the* investigative reporter on race matters in the South. Huie had overcome his fears—he told the story of actually stopping by the roadside as he was driving to Mississippi and vomiting in the ditch—and through exercising the courage to deal with men he knew to be murderers and the courage to risk criticism for paying these men cash for their sordid stories, Huie had brought the truth to light. There was probably no other way that the facts in the Till case would ever have become known.

It is not surprising therefore, that when the three young civil rights workers, Mickey Schwerner, James Chaney, and Andy Goodman, turned up missing on June 21, 1964, *The New York Herald Tribune* called Huie at once and asked him to drive to Philadelphia, Neshoba County, Mississippi, to get the story. Huie brought all the right tools to the job. A native Southerner, with the right accent and a ready smile, Huie could interview anyone, from blue-collar workers to the governor of the state. He was not an outsider, not a Yankee agitator, and people in Philadelphia opened up to him. He had honed his interview techniques in the preparation of a dozen books and, using what he had learned in the Till case, he was willing to spread a little cash around to find out what he wanted to know.

Huie had also developed some organizational techniques which he employed in Philadelphia. He knew that readers all over the United States and, as it turned out, all over the world, would want to know from his book more than they would learn from newspaper accounts. They would want to know what happened, but also *why* these events took place, and Huie knew readers wanted human faces put on the participants, especially the three victims.

He tackled the "why" first, by opening his book with the story of the cruel, violent, and senseless castration of Edward Aaron, an African American chosen at random so a Klansman could "prove himself" as a would-be mafioso "makes his bones." Once the reader has seen the Klan at work in the Aaron case, the murders in Mississippi, "for no good reason," do not seem so far-fetched.

Most importantly, however, at a time before Tom Wolfe, Gay Talese, and others were creating in New York City "The New Journalism," Huie was practicing it in Alabama. Huie employs in *Three Lives* the techniques of scenic construction, extensive use of dialogue acquired in many thorough interviews, and an authorial presence. These were only possible because Huie did the work. He traveled to New York to interview Mickey Schwerner's family, his widow, his friends from college and his colleagues at the social welfare center, Hamilton-Madison House, where Schwerner had worked prior to joining the Movement. Huie created characters on the page. Newspaper reporters wrote of three basically anonymous victims. Huie fleshed out Mickey Schwerner and, to a lesser extent, James Chaney and Andy Goodman, until they became people the readers felt they knew.

Having used the devices of fiction, however, to give his narrative drama and a human face, Huie never forgot that he was after the truth. To create the effect of accuracy and documentation in his books, Huie liked to include primary materials, so in *Three Lives* one finds letters from several of the principals to family, friends, or bosses. One finds Ku Klux Klan propaganda leaflets, items from Mississippi newspapers and excerpts from speeches by President Lyndon Johnson and the governors of Mississippi and Alabama. Also included are brochures, published reports and even newspaper advertisements. This is nonfiction. These events really happened. The documentary evidence was, Huie felt, an important part in telling the story.

And after the rest of the reporters had come to town, attended press briefings, filed their stories, and returned to New York or Los Angeles, Huie stayed on, continued to dig, and presented his readers with the present account: thorough, accurate, as complete as he could make it, and packed with his own sense of outrage.

After *Three Lives*, Huie would only once more write of racial violence in the South in nonfiction. Immediately after the assassination of the Reverend Dr. Martin Luther King, Jr., Huie brought his talents to bear in the ways he had honed in Live Oak, Florida, and Money and Philadelphia, Mississippi. He went to Memphis, paid James Earl Ray $35,000 for his story, checked it out thoroughly and laboriously, including his movements for several months before the shooting, and concluded in *He Slew the Dreamer* (1968) that Ray had acted alone. It wasn't the conclusion that would pay off the best for Huie and his publisher, but he felt there was no conspiracy, and wouldn't even hint that there was.

Racial injustice was at the heart of Huie's 1967 novel, *The Klansman*, as well. This time, however, there was a violent reaction against Huie himself. Klansmen came to Huie's house in the night, drove around the block in trucks, jeering and screaming, and even burned a cross on his lawn. Huie demanded from Governor Albert Brewer of Alabama the same state trooper protection that ex-governor George Wallace was receiving on his national independent campaign for the U.S. presidency. Huie saw a symmetry in the opposites. In the event, Huie hired an armed guard, and the two men stood watch over the house with automatic shotguns for a number of nights until the Klan interest moved on.

From 1970 until his death in 1986, Huie continued to write, but his work never again had the power of his works either about the First Great Crusade, WWII, or the Second Great Crusade, the Civil Rights movement. He published *In the Hours of the Night* in 1975, based loosely on the life and death of James V. Forrestal, WWII Secretary of the Navy and later Secretary of Defense. *Hours* was to have been the first of a trilogy of novels, the second set in Vietnam, and the third to deal with the Watergate conspiracy. (The second and third novels were never written.) This was followed by a pair of minor works of nonfiction, *A New Life to Live: Jimmy Putnam's Story* (1977) and *It's Me O Lord!* (1979).

Ruth Huie, Bill's wife, died in 1973 after a long, painful, and expensive bat-tle with cancer. In 1977 Huie married Martha Hunt Robertson, but there were no children with either Ruth or Martha. Huie's health began to fail in the 1980s, and he died on November 20, 1986, in Guntersville, Alabama. At the time of his death he was writing his memoirs, alternately titled *Report from Buck's Pocket* and *Recollections of a Loner*. At the time of his death, all twenty-one of Huie's works were out of print, but this edition of *Three Lives for Mississippi* will be the fifth book to be reissued in the past four years and with-out doubt there will be many more. Huie does more than inform the reader: whether he writes of Iwo Jima or Philadelphia, Mississippi, to read Huie's account is to be there.

Donald Noble
Professor of English
The University of Alabama

Index